FRESH
FROM
FLORIDA

Gulf Publishing Company
Houston, Texas

FRESH
FROM
FLORIDA

Six Decades of Recipes . . . Featuring Everyone's Favorite Fruits

Diana Gonzalez Kirby

FRESH
FROM
FLORIDA

Gulf Publishing Company
Book Division
P.O. Box 2608 □ Houston, Texas 77252-2608

10 9 8 7 6 5 4 3 2 1

Library of Congress Cataloging-in-Publication Data

Gonzalez Kirby, Diana.
    Fresh from Florida : six decades of recipes featuring every-
one's favorite fruits / Diana Gonzalez Kirby.
        p.   cm.
    Includes index.
    ISBN 0-88415-292-8
    1. Cookery (Fruit)   2. Fruit—Florida.   I. Title.
TX811.G64   1996
641.6'4–dc20   95-52701
                                                            CIP

Printed in the United States of America.

Contents

Acknowledgments

I would like to thank the following people and institutions for assisting me in the preparation of this work: Sandra H. Pate at the State of Florida Department of Citrus, Christina Phipps at the Florida Department of Agriculture & Consumer Services, Julia Graddy at the University of Florida Institute of Food and Agricultural Sciences, Becky Smith, Dawn Hugh, and Natalie Brown at the Historical Association of Southern Florida, William Brown at the University of Miami Archives and Special Collections Department in the Otto G. Richter Library, and Daniel Blazek at the Dante B. Fascell Department of Government Documents at the University of Miami Library. Frank Rodgers, Director of Libraries at the University of Miami, was instrumental in securing funds for reproducing the wonderful photographs that appear throughout the book.

For encouragement, moral support, and camaraderie, my thanks go to my good friend, Margaret Borgeest. This book is dedicated to Riley and Betty Anne.

FRESH
FROM
FLORIDA

Introduction

Miles of pristine beaches, opportunities in commercial and residential real estate, and Disney World are traditional themes that have been used to attract tourists and businesses to Florida. In much the same way, the Florida Department of Agriculture, the Citrus Commission, and the Florida Department of Natural Resources have used recipes to encourage seasonal visitors as well as permanent residents to buy and consume Florida-grown fruits and vegetables.

Fresh from Florida is designed to appeal to the health-conscious consumer by featuring many low-fat recipes. But the book also provides a window into the historical, cultural, and economic development of Florida regional cuisine.

Fresh from Florida contains recipes featured in promotional publications from the Florida Department of Agriculture, the Florida Citrus Commission, the Florida Department of Citrus, the Florida Department of Natural Resources, the University of Florida Agricultural Extension Service, and the United States Government Printing Office. The publications span a sixty-year period and reflect a period of growth in Florida's agricultural and tourism sectors.

The book brings together in one place a wide variety of recipes for beverages, breads, cakes, cookies, desserts, entrees, fruit cups, pies, salads, soups, stews, and sauces that were previously published in several sources over a span of six decades. As such, this cookbook differs from others in that it presents a historic and "folksy" overview of Florida regional cuisine based on recipes that were originally developed by government agencies to promote locally grown produce.

Motoring thru palm bordered orange groves in tropical Florida. Chicago: C.T. Art-Colortone, no date. Florida Postcard Collection, Archives and Special Collections Department, University of Miami Library.

Citrus Preparation Tips

Here are some quick, easy and versatile preparation tips from the Florida Department of Citrus that will help you brighten your recipes with Florida citrus:

1. Florida Orange Smiles

Do not peel orange. Slice orange in half crosswise. From each half, slice diagonally to get three or four smiles. Eat sections straight off the peel. Just pull down on both ends, and the fruit will pop up, just waiting to be eaten.

Smiles are a colorful and nutritious treat for any occasion. They travel neatly in school, office, and picnic lunches.

2. Picture-Perfect Sections and Rounds

Chill fruit before peeling. Using sharp knife, cut through rind and membrane using round strokes in spiral fashion. Trim off remaining pieces of membrane after peeling.

For sections, cut with sharp knife alongside, but not on, each dividing membrane to core.

Wedges should be membrane-free on all sides, with dividing membrane hidden inside each wedge.

For round slices, start at top of fruit and slice through circumference.

The surprisingly simple secret of removing the white pith opens up endless possibilities for enjoying fresh Florida citrus. Sections and rounds are ideal for dazzling salads, sweet and savory sauces, desserts and other dishes.

3. **Florida Grapefruit Points**

Slice grapefruit in half through stem end. Take one half and place cut side down. Cut this half in half (through stem end). Keep these halves together and slice the other way, across the previous cuts. Perfect points will fall right out; repeat with remaining half.

Like smiles, points are bite size, perfectly portable, and fun and easy to eat.

Source: *Florida Citrus Cooking: Recipes from the Sunshine State.* Tallahassee: Florida Department of Citrus, 1994.

4. **Grapefruit Sections**

The former Florida Citrus Commission recommends cutting grapefruit into sections for use in salads and fruit cups as follows:

Chill fruit before preparing. To section, cut off peel in strips from top to bottom, cutting deep enough to remove white membrane. Then cut slices from top and bottom. Go over fruit again, removing any remaining white membrane. Cut along side of each dividing membrane from outside to middle of core. Remove section by section, over a bowl, to retain juice from fruit. If desired, sections may be sprinkled lightly with sugar.

Grapefruit sections are a brand-new treat when used to fill the center of baked acorn squash. Sprinkle each half with a tablespoon of brown sugar and dot with butter. Add sections during the last 15 minutes of baking.

Top broiled fish the last 10 minutes of broiling with grapefruit sections. Sprinkle with paprika and dot with butter.

Add three or four grapefruit sections to red cabbage when cooking. The acid of the fruit aids in retaining the appetizing color. When cabbage is tender, add more grapefruit sections, and heat to serving temperature.

In cooking Swiss steaks and pot roasts, use grapefruit juice as part of the liquid for interesting flavor.

Source: *Florida Citrus Fare*. Lakeland, FL: Florida Citrus Commission, no date.

Beverages

Private tea served by Sergeant Stanford on board H.M.S. Danae, Miami, March 4, 1932. Floyd and Marion Rinhart Collection, Archives and Special Collections, University of Miami Library.

Afternoon Tea

3 teaspoons of tea
2 cups of boiling water
1 lime
Cloves
Sprigs of mint

Make the tea in teapot or with tea ball; let stand for several minutes; then serve, placing in each cup a slice of lime pierced with a clove. Sweeten to taste.

Source: *Florida Fruits and Vegetables in the Family Menu.* Bulletin No. 46, New Series, Tallahassee, FL: Florida Department of Agriculture, 1956.

Blueberry Benchpress

1 ounce orange juice
3 ounces blueberry compote or puree
1 ounce frozen strawberries (thawed)
2 ounces margarita mix
1 ounce pineapple juice
1 rounded 8-ounce scoop of crushed ice

Combine ingredients in blender. Blend for 60 seconds.

Source: *Drinks to Health; Fresh Alternatives to Alcoholic Drinks Featuring Florida Orange and Grapefruit Juices.* Lakeland, FL: Florida Department of Citrus, no date.

Citrus Cocktail

¼ cup lemon juice
¼ cup grapefruit juice
¼ cup orange juice
¼ cup sugar dissolved in water
Few grains of salt
Cracked ice
Mint sprigs

Combine fruit juices, sugar, salt, and water. Pour over cracked ice in glasses and serve garnished with mint sprigs.

Source: *Florida Fruits and Vegetables in the Family Menu.* Bulletin No. 46, New Series, Tallahassee, FL: Florida Department of Agriculture, 1956.

Citus Sodas

For each soda, combine ⅔ cup chilled orange, tangerine, or blended orange and grapefruit juice with ⅓ cup chilled ginger ale in a tall glass. Add a large scoop of vanilla ice cream.

Source: *Florida Citrus Fare*. Lakeland, FL: Florida Citrus Commission, no date.

Flaming Florida Fruit Madeira

2 grapefruits
2 oranges
2 tangerines
1½ ounce Madeira wine
1½ ounce honey
1½ cup sugar
Nutmeg
Brandy

Cut fruit in half; remove pulp by cutting around each section, removing membrane. Mix all fruit sections and marinate in the Madeira wine, honey and sugar for two hours. Reserve grapefruit and orange halves, sprinkle a little nutmeg in each. Place under hot broiler for three minutes; now fill cups with marinated fruit and broil another five minutes. Add 1 teaspoon brandy to each serving, flame and serve immediately. Use orange cups for smaller serving.

Source: *Famous Florida Chefs' Favorite Citrus Recipes*. Lakeland, FL: Florida Citrus Commission, no date.

Florida Champagne

1 cup sugar
3 cups water
4 cups cranberry juice, chilled
4 cups pineapple juice, chilled
2 cups orange juice, chilled
2 liters ginger ale, chilled
Orange slices
Cherries

In a medium saucepan, combine sugar and water; boil for 3 minutes. Chill. In a large punch bowl, combine chilled juices and sugar-water mixture. To add color to cranberry punch, prepare an ice ring using ginger ale, orange slices and cherries; freeze. When ready to serve, add ginger ale to juices and place ice ring in punch bowl.

40 half-cup servings.

Source: *Florida Holiday Recipes.* Tallahassee, FL: Florida Department of Agriculture and Consumer Services, 1990.

Florida Citrus Spritz

4 ounces orange juice
4 ounces club soda
Squeeze of lemon

Combine ingredients. Pour over crushed or shaved ice in 10-ounce glass. Garnish with orange slice or twist, if desired.

Source: *Drinks to Health; Fresh Alternatives to Alcoholic Drinks Featuring Florida Orange and Grapefruit Juices.* Lakeland, FL: Florida Department of Citrus, no date.

Florida Derby Daiquiri

½ ounce fresh lime juice
1 ounce fresh orange juice
Scant teaspoon sugar
1½ ounce white rum
1 cup crushed ice

Mix all in blender 10 seconds. Serve unstrained in chilled cocktail glass.

Source: *Famous Florida Chefs' Favorite Citrus Recipes.* Lakeland, FL: Florida Citrus Commission. no date.

Florida Limeade

⅓ cup sugar
1 cup water
6 limes
Finely crushed ice
Carbonated or plain water
Mint

Combine sugar and water in a saucepan; place over heat and stir until sugar is dissolved; cool. Cut limes in half; juice. Add juice to sugar syrup; divide mixture into 6 tall glasses. Fill to top with crushed ice. Pour in carbonated or plain water; stir. Garnish with mint sprigs and lime slices.

To frost edge of glass, dip rim in egg white, then in granulated sugar. Put in refrigerator to chill and harden frosted edge.

6 servings.

Source: *Florida's Favorite Foods. Fruits and Vegetables in the Family Menu.* Bulletin No. 46, Tallahassee, FL: Florida Department of Agriculture, 1959.

Florida Orange Sauce Flambé

2 cups orange sections, drained
2 tablespoons of butter
2 tablespoons of brown sugar
½ teaspoon cinnamon
1½ bananas, peeled and sliced
⅓ cup rum
⅓ cup brandy
Vanilla ice cream

Melt butter in saucepan. Stir in brown sugar, add cinnamon, sliced bananas, and drained orange sections. Stir in rum and heat thoroughly. Slowly pour brandy over sauce and light flame. Spoon sauce over ice cream.

6 servings.

Source: *Famous Florida Chefs' Favorite Citrus Recipes.* Lakeland, FL: Florida Citrus Commission, no date.

Florida Stars

6 ounces grapefruit juice, pink or white
1 sweet carambola (star fruit), peeled and seeded
Splash of soda
½ ounce grenadine

Combine ingredients in blender. Blend until smooth. Serve over ice. Garnish with grapefruit point and star fruit, if desired.

Source: *Drinks to Health; Fresh Alternatives to Alcoholic Drinks Featuring Florida Orange and Grapefruit Juices.* Lakeland, FL: Florida Department of Citrus, no date.

Florida Sunshine

8 ounces orange juice
Splash of grenadine

Pour orange juice in goblet first and then top with a splash of grenadine. Do not stir. Serve immediately. Garnish with orange slice and a mint sprig.

Source: *Florida Citrus Sampler.* Lakeland, FL: Florida Department of Citrus, no date.

Florida Sunshine Shake

1 cup orange juice
½ cup grapefruit juice
1 ripe banana
½ cup low-fat vanilla yogurt
½ teaspoon vanilla extract

Combine all ingredients in blender until smooth. Pour into glass, and serve immediately.

Makes two 8-ounce servings.

Source: *Florida Citrus Cooking: Recipes from the Sunshine State.* Tallahassee, FL: Florida Department of Citrus, 1994.

Florida Toddy

2 cups orange juice
1 cup cranberry juice cocktail
¼ cup sugar
1 teaspoon whole cloves
1 3-inch piece stick cinnamon
1 teaspoon grated orange rind
6 orange slices

Combine all ingredients except orange slices in saucepan. Place over low heat, bring to boiling point; simmer 5 minutes; strain. Pour into heated bowl or pitcher. Stud orange slices with additional cloves; float on top.

6 servings.

Source: *Florida Citrus Fare.* Lakeland, FL: Florida Citrus Commission, no date.

Fontainebleau Fruit Punch

½ gallon orange juice
6 ounces grapefruit juice
1 64-ounce can pineapple juice
8 ounces sour mix
4 ounces grenadine

Combine ingredients. Garnish with orange and grapefruit slices or wheels, if desired.

1 gallon.

Source: *Drinks to Health; Fresh Alternatives to Alcoholic Drinks Featuring Florida Orange and Grapefruit Juices.* Lakeland, FL: Florida Department of Citrus, no date.

Frozen Floridian

2 ounces grapefruit juice
2 ounces orange juice
2 ounces strawberries, fresh or frozen
2 teaspoons superfine sugar
1 ounce grenadine
1 ounce half & half

Combine ingredients in blender. Pour into 12-ounce stemmed, footed wine glass. Garnish with whipped cream, cherry and orange slice or orange rind, if desired.

Source: *Drinks to Health; Fresh Alternatives to Alcoholic Drinks Featuring Florida Orange and Grapefruit Juices.* Lakeland, FL: Florida Department of Citrus, no date.

Fruity Florida Daiquiri

4 ounces orange juice
1 kiwi, peeled
1½ ounces strawberry fruit puree
1 scoop crushed ice

Combine ingredients in blender. Blend until smooth. Pour over ice. Garnish with orange slices or orange twists, if desired.

Source: *Drinks to Health; Fresh Alternatives to Alcoholic Drinks Featuring Florida Orange and Grapefruit Juices.* Lakeland, FL: Florida Department of Citrus, no date.

Entrance to the Garnet Orange Grove, St. Augustine, 1923. Floyd and Marion Rinhart Collection, Archives and Special Collections, University of Miami Library.

Grapefruit Ponce de Leon

¾ cup grapefruit juice
¼ cup honey

Mix grapefruit and honey. Place in refrigerator overnight. Serve.

Source: *Florida Fruits and Vegetables in the Family Menu.* Bulletin No. 46, New Series, Tallahassee, FL: Florida Department of Agriculture, 1956.

Grapefruit Whitecaps

3¼ cups canned or fresh grapefruit juice
1 egg white
2 tablespoons sugar
Nutmeg

Pour chilled juice into tall glasses. Beat egg white until stiff; beat in sugar gradually. Put spoonful in each glass; sprinkle with nutmeg.

4 servings.

Source: *Florida Citrus Fare.* Lakeland, FL: Florida Citrus Commission, no date.

Guava Honey Punch

1 cup honey
2 cups pared and seeded guavas and juice
2 cups water
¼ cup lemon juice
½ cup orange juice
Mineral or ice water

Simmer honey and water together until blended, set aside to cool. Force guavas through fruit press and combine the pulp with orange and lemon juice. Add to the cold syrup and chill thoroughly. Just before serving, strain and dilute to taste with mineral or ice water. Peaches, plums, or mangoes may be used the same way as guavas.

Source: *Florida Honey and Its Hundred Uses.* Bulletin No. 66, Tallahassee, FL: Florida Department of Agriculture, 1955.

Hollywood Honey Punch

Juice 12 lemons
Juice 12 oranges
3 quarts water
1 pint tamarind juice
1 pint guava juice
1 pint shredded pineapple
Honey to sweeten

Warm honey and add to water. Blend and add fruit juices and shredded pineapple and chill. When ready to serve garnish with thin slices of lemon and orange and pour over ice.

Source: *Florida Honey and Its Hundred Uses.* Bulletin No. 66, Tallahassee, FL: Florida Department of Agriculture, 1933.

Honey Orange Cocktail

Mix juice of 6 oranges, 6 tablespoons honey, and a few grains of salt. When ready to serve, shake up with ice cubes and add shreds of yellow orange rind. Decorate with sprig of mint.

Source: *Florida Honey and Its Hundred Uses.* Bulletin No. 66, Tallahassee, FL: Florida Department of Agriculture, 1933.

Hot Honey Lemonade

Mix 4 tablespoons lemon juice with 4 tablespoons honey. Add 1 cup boiling water. Drink hot.

Source: *Florida Honey and Its Hundred Uses.* Bulletin No. 66, Tallahassee, FL: Florida Department of Agriculture, 1955.

International Minted Fruit Melange

1 cup membrane-free orange sections
1 cup cubed pears
1 cup cubed pineapple
3 teaspoons sugar
2 tablespoons chopped after-dinner mints

Combine fruit. Sprinkle with sugar and mints, chill and serve.

4 servings.

Source: *Famous Florida Chefs' Favorite Citrus Recipes.* Lakeland, FL: Florida Citrus Commission, no date.

Lime Juice Cocktail

4 tablespoons lime juice
2 tablespoons orange juice
2 tablespoons sugar syrup
⅓ cup ginger ale
Crushed ice

Place ingredients in shaker; shake, and pour over crushed ice into four glasses.

Source: *Florida Fruits and Vegetables in the Family Menu.* Bulletin No. 46, New Series, Tallahassee, FL: Florida Department of Agriculture, 1956.

Melon-Peach Cocktail

Fill half a small cantaloupe (chilled) with sliced peaches. In the center fill with seeded grapes, blueberries, or blackberries. Sprinkle freely with lemon and orange juice combined or with slightly sweetened lemon juice.

Source: *Florida Fruits and Vegetables in the Family Menu.* Bulletin No. 46, New Series, Tallahassee, FL: Florida Department of Agriculture, 1956.

Orange Brulot (Creole Style)

1 orange, thin skin, wash and dry. Plunge into hot water for 5 minutes.
1½ ounce of cognac
1 lump of sugar

Using a sharp knife, cut orange in half. Remove pulp of orange by inserting edge of thin spoon between skin and pulp. Work around entire half of orange to separate. Carefully roll skin from pulp, turning it inside out, then turn and use this skin for cup. Place on lower half of orange. Fill cup with the cognac. Place lump of sugar in a teaspoon filled with cognac and ignite. When sugar begins to color, gently float onto surface of cognac in orange cup. When flame flickers, blow out and serve.

Source: *Famous Florida Chefs' Favorite Citrus Recipes.* Lakeland, FL: Florida Citrus Commission, no date.

Orange Freeze

1 8-ounce glass fresh orange juice
1 scoop orange sherbet
Dash of grenadine
Sections of sliced oranges

Whip in blender until thick and creamy.

Source: *Famous Florida Chefs' Favorite Citrus Recipes.* Lakeland, FL: Florida Citrus Commission, no date.

Orange Juice Cocktail

4 small oranges
Few grains of salt
1 teaspoon lemon juice
½ cup strawberries
½ cup crushed pineapple
Sugar to taste

Cut a thin slice from the tops of oranges. Remove pulp and juice. Add strawberries, lemon juice and sugar to pulp and juice of oranges. Fill peel and set on ice and leave until thoroughly cold. Serve in glasses surrounded with crushed ice.

Source: *Florida Fruits and Vegetables in the Family Menu.* Bulletin No. 46, New Series, Tallahassee, FL: Florida Department of Agriculture, 1956.

Orange Mango Slush

6 ounces orange juice
½ mango, peeled
3 ounces cranberry juice
Splash lemon-lime soda
1 ounce crushed ice

Combine ingredients in blender. Blend until smooth. Garnish with orange points, mango slices, and a cherry, if desired.

Source: *Drinks to Health; Fresh Alternatives to Alcoholic Drinks Featuring Florida Orange and Grapefruit Juices.* Lakeland, FL: Florida Department of Citrus, no date.

Orange Peachsicle

---

2 ounces orange juice
2 ounces peach daiquiri mix
1 teaspoon almond-flavored syrup

Combine ingredients in blender. Garnish with orange wedge and a twist of lime, or top with whipped cream, if desired.

Source: *Drinks to Health; Fresh Alternatives to Alcoholic Drinks Featuring Florida Orange and Grapefruit Juices.* Lakeland, FL: Florida Department of Citrus, no date.

Palace Punch

---

4 ounces orange juice
4 ounces pineapple juice
2 ounces pina colada mix
Splash of grenadine

Combine ingredients. Pour into 12-ounce collins glass, packed with cubed ice. Garnish with orange slice or twist and cherry or strawberry, if desired.

Source: *Drinks to Health; Fresh Alternatives to Alcoholic Drinks Featuring Florida Orange and Grapefruit Juices.* Lakeland, FL: Florida Department of Citrus, no date.

Papaya Cocktail

Dice papaya and serve in glasses with orange, lemon, or lime juice, and a little sugar and chipped ice.

Source: *Florida's Favorite Foods. Fruits and Vegetables in the Family Menu.* Bulletin No. 46, Tallahassee, FL: Florida Department of Agriculture, 1959.

Papaya Shake

2 cups mashed ripe papaya pulp
⅛ cup lemon or ¼ cup lime juice
⅔ cup sugar
1½ cups evaporated milk
1½ cups water
1 teaspoon nutmeg

Combine mashed fruit and sugar, add other ingredients, chill. Just before serving, shake with cracked ice in a glass jar.

Source: *Florida Fruit and Vegetable Recipes.* Tallahassee, FL: Florida Department of Agriculture, no date.

Peach Cocktail

Place 4 tablespoons of fresh cubed peaches in cocktail glasses. Add 4 tablespoons of grape, pineapple or any berry juice. Sprinkle with nut meats. Fill dish with shaved ice. Serve.

Source: *Florida Fruits and Vegetables in the Family Menu.* Bulletin No. 46, New Series, Tallahassee, FL: Florida Department of Agriculture, 1956.

Strawberry Citrus Punch

10 cups (80 ounces) lemon-lime carbonated beverage, chilled and
   divided
Lime slices
Orange slices
Strawberry slices
6 cups strawberries
1 6-ounce container frozen limeade concentrate
¾ cup unsweetened pineapple juice
¾ cup orange juice
2 tablespoons lime juice

Ice ring: Combine 4 cups of lemon-lime beverage with lime, orange, and strawberry slices; pour into mold and freeze overnight. Remove stems and caps from strawberries. Puree berries, 3 cups at a time, in a food processor. Transfer berries to punch bowl. Add limeade concentrate and fruit juices; stir. Cover and chill until ready to serve. Add remaining lemon-lime beverage and ice ring at serving time.

20–24 servings.

Source: *Holiday Recipes Fresh from Florida.* Tallahassee, FL: Florida Department of Agriculture and Consumer Services, no date.

Summer Breeze

4 ounces grapefruit juice
2 ounces lemon-lime soda
1 ounce cranberry juice

Combine ingredients. Serve over crushed ice packed in a collins glass. Garnish with grapefruit point, if desired.

Source: *Drinks to Health; Fresh Alternatives to Alcoholic Drinks Featuring Florida Orange and Grapefruit Juices.* Lakeland, FL: Florida Department of Citrus, no date.

Sunshine Sundae

½ cup Temple orange or tangerine pieces, peeled and sliced/segmented
1 teaspoon honey
¾ cup lowfat vanilla frozen yogurt
2 teaspoons chopped walnuts

Mix sliced Temple orange with honey, and dollop onto frozen yogurt. Top with walnuts.

Makes 1 serving.

Source: *Florida Citrus Cooking: Recipes from the Sunshine State.* Tallahassee, FL: Florida Department of Citrus, 1994.

The Sunshiner

Into a shaker put cracked ice, ½ jigger triple sec, ¾ jigger galliano, and fresh orange juice. Shake well and pour into champagne glass.

Source: *Famous Florida Chefs' Favorite Citrus Recipes.* Lakeland, FL: Florida Citrus Commission, no date.

Tropical Cooler

8 ounces guava juice
Juice of ½ fresh lime
Cracked ice
Honey to taste

Blend well and serve with thin slices of fruit.

Source: *Florida Honey and Its Hundred Uses.* Bulletin No. 66, Tallahassee, FL: Florida Department of Agriculture, 1933.

Tropical Tidbit

Fill sherbet glass with grapefruit sections and juice to within ½ inch of top. Insert thin slices of cantaloupe or melon. Top with lime ice or sherbet.

Source: *Chilled Florida Citrus Sections For Around the Year Profit.* CCS-1, Lakeland, FL: Florida Citrus Commission, no date.

Fruit Cups

Blueberry Compote

1 pint blueberries
⅓ cup granulated sugar
3 tablespoons brown sugar
¼ cup water
1 pint raspberries

Cook granulated sugar and water for three minutes. Add blueberries and cook about four minutes. Cool and then chill. Place raspberries in a serving dish or arrange in individual bowls and sprinkle with brown sugar. Pour blueberries over raspberries and serve.

Source: *Florida Blueberries.* Bulletin No. 13-B, New Series, Tallahassee, FL: Florida Department of Agriculture, 1950.

A bunch of Indian River oranges. Copyright, 1891, by George Barker. New York: Underwood & Underwood. Floyd and Marion Rinhart Collection, Archives and Special Collections, University of Miami Library.

Fiesta Cup

Combine orange and grapefruit sections with avocado and melon balls. Top with a swirl of whipped cream topping and garnish with grapes.

Source: *Chilled Florida Citrus Sections for Around the Year Profit.* CCS-1, Lakeland, FL: Florida Citrus Commission, no date.

Florida Melon Cocktail

2 3-ounce packages strawberry or raspberry gelatin mix
1 cup boiling water
1 cup watermelon pulp with seeds removed
1 cup watermelon juice
2 teaspoons lime juice

Add boiling water to gelatin. Stir to dissolve completely. Place watermelon in blender until liquified or force through a sieve. Strain to obtain the watermelon juice. Add watermelon juice and lime juice to gelatin. Pour into mold. Chill until slightly thickened. Fold in watermelon pulp. Chill until set. Unmold on plate of escarole or endive. Garnish with mayonnaise and watermelon balls.

6 to 8 servings.

Source: *Florida Red Ripe Watermelons.* Tallahassee, FL: Florida Department of Agriculture, no date.

Fruit Cup No. 1

Combination 1: Grapefruit sections with sliced bananas and diced apple (leave red peel on for color contrast).

Combination 2: Grapefruit and orange sections with finely cut dates and shredded coconut.

Combination 3: Grapefruit sections with diced avocado and chopped pimiento.

Combination 4: Grapefruit sections with sliced strawberries.

Combination 5: Top grapefruit sections with orange or lime sherbet. Garnish with mint sprigs.

Source: *Florida Citrus Fare.* Lakeland, FL: Florida Citrus Commission, no date.

Fruit Cup No. 2

Remove all membrane from sections of chilled grapefruit, arranging the sections in a wheel on a dessert plate, then pour hot chocolate sauce over the fruit just before serving. Maraschino juice used to sweeten grapefruit served in the shell imparts a delicate color and flavor. No sugar is needed in this case. Try crushed maple sugar or honey for sweetening instead of sugar.

Source: *Florida Fruits and Vegetables in the Family Menu.* Bulletin No. 46, New Series, Tallahassee, FL: Florida Department of Agriculture, 1956.

Fruit Cup No. 3

3 large oranges
2 slices pineapple, diced
12 marshmallows, quartered
⅓ cup broken nut meats
⅔ cup strawberries (halved)
Lettuce leaves

Cut oranges in half, remove pulp carefully, leaving shells clean. Mix pineapple, marshmallows, nuts, and strawberries with orange pulp. Fill orange cups, garnish with nuts. Serve on lettuce.

Source: *Florida Fruits and Vegetables in the Family Menu.* Bulletin No. 46, New Series, Tallahassee, FL: Florida Department of Agriculture, 1956.

Fruit Cup No. 4

3 oranges
¼ cup honey
2 bananas
1 cup pineapple chunks
½ cup shredded coconut

Section oranges. Add sliced bananas and pineapple. Add honey, mix gently. Spoon into 6 serving dishes and top each with shredded coconut.

Source: *Using Florida Citrus Fruits.* Circular No. 231, Gainesville, FL: University of Florida Agricultural Extension Service, 1962.

Fruit Cup No. 5

½ cup orange juice

2 tablespoons lemon juice

2 tablespoons pineapple syrup

Sugar

¾ cup orange pieces

¾ cup diced pineapple

¾ cup of one of the following fruits: white grapes, strawberries,
peaches, pears, cantaloupes, bananas

Combine fruit juices and sweeten to taste, keeping rather tart. Add mixed fruits. Place on ice. Serve very cold in cocktail or sherbet glasses. Garnish each serving with Surinam cherry, strawberry, carissa cut in half, or loquat slices. Use mint if fruits are not in season.

Oranges should have all membrane removed. If grapes are used, seeds should be removed. If strawberries are used, cut in half. Peaches or pears, if used, should be diced; cherries should be stoned; cantaloupe or bananas should be cut in balls or small sections.

Source: *Florida Fruits and Vegetables in the Family Menu.* Bulletin No. 46, New Series, Tallahassee, FL: Florida Department of Agriculture, 1956.

Prize pineapple from Musa Isle Fruit Farm, Miami, Fla. Florida Postcard Collection, Archives and Special Collections, University of Miami Library.

Pear Boats in an Orange Sea

1 16-ounce can Bartlett pears, drained
Juice of 3 large oranges

Put into a shallow bowl and chill. Pears absorb the orange flavor. Dress up with whipped cream and cherries if desired. Be sure to save pear juice to combine with grapefruit juice or sections or with other citrus combinations.

6 servings.

Source: *Florida's Favorite Recipes for Citrus Fruits. A compilation of recipes which won top honors in county contests jointly sponsored by the Florida Agricultural Extension Service, home demonstration work, and the Florida Chain Store Council as a feature of Florida's "Eat More Citrus Month," February, 1954.* Lakeland, FL: Florida Citrus Commission, 1954.

Watermelon Snacks

Insert toothpicks into melon cubes or balls. Roll in confectioners' sugar, place on foil, and freeze 1 hour. Or, dip melon balls into honey and then into toasted coconut.

Source: *Florida Red Ripe Watermelons*. Tallahassee, FL: Florida Department of Agriculture, no date.

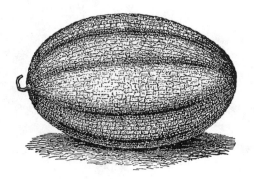

Breads

Blueberry Muffins

2 tablespoons butter
¾ cup sugar
1 tablespoon salt
2½ cups flour
2 eggs
1½ cups milk
1½ cups blueberries
3 tablespoons baking powder

Cream butter and sugar; add slightly beaten eggs, 2 cups of the flour mixed with salt, alternately with the milk, and then the baking powder. Roll the berries in ½ cup of flour, and add them last. Fill greased muffin pans half full and bake in oven 25 minutes at 350 degrees.

Source: *Florida Blueberries.* Bulletin No. 13-B, New Series, Tallahassee, FL: Florida Department of Agriculture, 1950.

Cinnamon Fruit Toast

6 slices of bread
¼ cup grapefruit juice
Grated rind of grapefruit
Powdered sugar
1 egg
1 cup sugar
2 slices oranges

Beat egg with lemon and grapefruit juice until well blended, then add sugar that has been mixed with the grated grapefruit rind and beat well. Cut circles from the bread slices and dip in the egg mixture. Fry in a buttered pan until golden brown on both sides. Cover with orange slices, sift with powdered sugar, and serve immediately. (To prepare oranges, peel, taking with it all the white membrane. With a thin, sharp knife, cut the orange into thin strips lengthwise).

Source: *Florida Fruits and Vegetables in the Family Menu.* Bulletin No. 46, New Series, Tallahassee, FL: Florida Department of Agriculture, 1956.

Crepes with Grapefruit Maple Sauce

1 cup milk
¾ cup water
3 egg yolks
1½ cups sifted flour
5 tablespoons butter or margarine, melted
¼ teaspoon salt
2 tablespoons chopped chives
Vegetable oil for frying

In container of electric blender or food processor, combine all ingredients except chives and oil; blend 1 minute, or until smooth. Stir in chives. Refrigerate 2 hours or overnight. Lightly brush a 6- or 7-inch crepe pan or skillet with oil. Place over moderately-high heat until a drop or water bounces on the surface. Remove skillet from heat; pour 3 tablespoons batter into center of skillet. Tilt skillet to spread batter evenly, return to heat. Cook 1 minute, or until bottom is lightly browned. Slide spatula under crepe; turn to brown other side. Turn crepe out onto waxed paper. Repeat steps with remaining batter.

Sauce

¼ cup butter or margarine
1 tablespoon cornstarch
½ cup grapefruit juice
¼ cup maple syrup
1 grapefruit, peeled and sectioned

In medium saucepan melt ¼ cup butter; whisk in cornstarch. Whisk in grapefruit juice and maple syrup; bring to a boil. Continue boiling, stirring constantly, 1 minute, until slightly thickened. Remove from heat; add grapefruit sections. Arrange crepes on serving plates. Serve with grapefruit sauce.

18 six-inch crepes.

Source: *Taste the Tropics with Florida Grapefruit.* Lakeland, FL: Florida Department of Citrus, no date.

Eloise Muffins

Sweeten and drain pulp of 1 grapefruit. Cream ½ cup shortening, add ½ cup sugar. Beat 2 eggs—add to shortening mixture. Add 1 cup milk. Sift 2 teaspoons baking powder with 3 cups flour and 1 teaspoon salt. Add ¼ teaspoon baking soda to 1 cup grapefruit pulp. Add to first mixture. Put in muffin tins. Bake ½ hour at 350 degrees.

Serves 16.

Source: *Florida Fruits and Vegetables in the Family Menu.* Bulletin No. 46, New Series, Tallahassee, FL: Florida Department of Agriculture, 1956.

English Muffins L'Orange

6 English muffins, split
6 eggs
½ cup orange juice
½ cup light cream
2 tablespoons butter

Beat 6 eggs, ½ cup orange juice, ½ cup light cream. Soak muffins, then fry in butter.

Sauce for toast

¼ cup Curaçao
1 cup orange juice
¼ cup sugar
30 orange sections

Bring orange juice to boil, thicken with corn starch and Curaçao. Garnish toast with orange sections, cover with sauce and brown sugar, sprinkle with coconut, and brown under broiler.

Source: *Famous Florida Chefs' Favorite Citrus Recipes.* Lakeland, FL: Florida Citrus Commission, no date.

Florida Biscuits

Add 2 teaspoons grated orange rind to standard biscuit mixture; use half milk, half orange juice for liquid. Dip a half lump of sugar in orange juice, then press into the top of each biscuit. When baked this makes a sweet glaze.

Source: *Florida Citrus Fare.* Lakeland, FL: Florida Citrus Commission, no date.

Florida Citrus Nut Bread

1 stick butter
¾ cup sugar
2 eggs
1¾ cups flour
¼ teaspoon salt
1 teaspoon baking powder
½ teaspoon baking soda
⅓ cup milk
2 teaspoons orange rind, grated
2 teaspoons grapefruit rind, grated
3 tablespoons orange juice
3 tablespoons grapefruit juice
1 teaspoon vanilla extract
1 cup pecans, chopped
½ cup powdered sugar

Preheat oven to 325 degrees. Cream butter and sugar. Beat in eggs; set aside.

Sift flour with salt, baking powder, and baking soda. Add to batter alternately with milk. Add grated rind and 2 tablespoons each of orange and grapefruit juice, reserving 1 tablespoon orange juice and 1 tablespoon grapefruit juice. Stir in vanilla and pecans.

Pour into a greased loaf pan and bake 45 minutes to an hour, until toothpick inserted in center comes out clean.

Mix remaining juices with powdered sugar. Remove bread from pan, poke holes in it with a fork and pour glaze over it. Let bread sit overnight wrapped in foil or plastic wrap to allow flavors to blend.

1 loaf.

Source: *Holiday Recipes Fresh from Florida.* Tallahassee, FL: Florida Department of Agriculture and Consumer Services, no date.

Florida Orange Bread

½ cup orange rind (3 oranges)
½ cup sugar
¼ cup water
1 tablespoons butter or margarine
1 cup orange juice
1 egg, well-beaten
2½ cups sifted all-purpose flour
3 teaspoons baking powder
¼ teaspoon soda
½ teaspoon salt

Wash oranges; dry. Remove the thin orange rind with a sharp knife, cutting around the orange; cut rind into very thin slivers with scissors. Combine sugar and water, add the rind; stir constantly over heat until the sugar is melted; cook slowly about 5 minutes. (The peel and syrup should measure ⅔ cup.) Add butter; stir until melted; add orange juice and beaten egg. Sift together into mixing bowl, flour, baking powder, soda and salt. Add orange mixture and mix just enough to moisten ingredients. (Batter should be lumpy.) Bake in greased loaf pan, 9½ × 4½ × 3 inches, in slow oven (325 degrees) for 1 hour and 15 minutes, or until done. Turn out on rack to cool.

1 loaf.

Source: *Florida Citrus Fare.* Lakeland, FL: Florida Citrus Commission, no date.

Florida Orange Date Nut Bran Muffins

2 cups shredded bran cereal

¾ cup boiling water

¼ cup vegetable oil

¾ cup buttermilk

¼ cup Florida orange juice

2 tablespoons dark molasses

2 tablespoons honey

1 tablespoon grated orange zest

1 large egg or egg substitute

¾ cup all-purpose flour

½ cup whole wheat flour

1½ teaspoons baking soda

½ teaspoon salt

1 cup chopped dates

¾ cup chopped walnuts

Heat oven to 400 degrees. Grease one 12-cup muffin tin. In a large bowl, combine bran cereal, water, and oil, stirring until bran softens. In a small bowl, whisk buttermilk, Florida orange juice, molasses, honey, orange zest, and egg until blended. In a small bowl, combine flours, baking soda and salt. Add buttermilk mixture to bran, stirring to combine. Add flour mixture, dates and walnuts to bran mixture, stirring just until flour is moistened. Spoon into muffin cups, and bake until top springs back when lightly pressed, about 18 minutes. Let cool in pan 5 minutes before removing to wire rack.

Makes 12 muffins.

Source: *Florida Citrus Cooking: Recipes from the Sunshine State.* Tallahassee, FL: Florida Department of Citrus, 1994.

Florida Orange Honey Butter

½ cup or 1 stick unsalted butter or margarine at room temperature
2 tablespoons honey
1 tablespoon grated orange zest

In a small bowl, beat butter until light and fluffy. Beat in honey and orange zest until well blended. Serve with muffins, pancakes or French toast.

Makes ½ cup.

Source: *Florida Citrus Cooking: Recipes from the Sunshine State.* Tallahassee, FL: Florida Department of Citrus, 1994.

Florida Orange Roll

3 eggs
1 cup sugar
6 tablespoons orange juice
1 cup sifted cake flour
1½ teaspoons baking powder
¼ teaspoon salt
Confectioners' sugar

Beat eggs until thick and lemon-colored; beat in sugar gradually. Blend in orange juice. Sift together flour, baking powder and salt; fold in. Line shallow pan, 10 × 15 inches, with wax paper, having the paper extend one inch beyond edge of pan. Turn batter into pan; bake in moderate oven (375 degrees) 20 minutes. Sift confectioners' sugar on brown wrapping paper 3 inches larger than pan. Turn cake out on this; remove wax paper. Spread with Florida Orange Filling and roll up like a jelly roll.

Florida Orange Filling

½ cup sugar
3 tablespoons cornstarch
¼ teaspoon salt
1¼ cups orange juice
1 egg yolk, slightly beaten
1 tablespoon butter or margarine

Combine sugar, cornstarch, and salt in top of double boiler. Blend in orange juice; mix thoroughly. Cook over direct heat and stir constantly until mixture is thickened. Place over boiling water; cook 10 minutes. Stir small amount orange mixture into the egg yolk; return to mixture in double boiler; cook, stirring constantly, 3 minutes longer. Add butter. Remove from heat; cool.

10 1-inch slices.

Source: *Florida Citrus Fare.* Lakeland, FL: Florida Citrus Commission, no date.

Florida Orange Sauce for Griddle Cakes and Waffles

Mix 1 tablespoon cornstarch, ½ cup sugar, and ¼ teaspooon salt; add 1 cup orange juice and 2 teaspoons grated orange rind. Bring to a boil, stirring constantly.

Source: *Florida Citrus Fare.* Lakeland, FL: Florida Citrus Commission, no date.

Florida Pancakes

2 egg yolks
½ teaspoon salt
½ teaspoon baking powder
2 tablespoons honey
2 cups orange sections chopped fine
1 cup sifted flour
2 egg whites stiffly beaten
Butter for frying

Beat the yolks, salt, and honey together, stir in orange sections and flour, and fold in beaten egg whites. Heat butter to cover bottom of skillet. Drop batter by tablespoons. Brown on both sides. Serve hot.

Serves 4.

Source: *Famous Florida Chefs' Favorite Citrus Recipes.* Lakeland, FL: Florida Citrus Commission, no date.

Glamour Biscuits

¼ to ½ cup butter or margarine
½ cup citrus marmalade
2 dozen small biscuits or 2 packages canned biscuits

Melt butter or margarine in shallow 9 × 13 inch baking pan. Dip biscuits in melted butter on both sides until completely coated. Press 1 teaspoon marmalade into center of each biscuit. Bake in a very hot oven, 450 degrees, 15 minutes or until brown.

Source: *Florida's Favorite Recipes for Citrus Fruits. A compilation of recipes which won top honors in county contests jointly sponsored by the Florida Agricultural Extension Service, home demonstration work, and the Florida Chain Store Council as a feature of Florida's "Eat More Citrus Month," February, 1954.* Lakeland, FL: Florida Citrus Commission, 1954.

Grapefruit Biscuits

2 cups sifted flour
2 teaspoons baking powder
½ teaspoon soda
½ teaspoon salt
6 tablespoons shortening
½ cup grapefruit juice
½ cup water

Sift flour, baking powder, soda, and salt together. Cut or rub in shortening until well blended. Slowly mix in grapefruit juice and water, using just enough to make dough that is soft but not sticky. Knead a few strokes. Roll or pat to ½ inch thickness. Cut with a 2½ inch cutter. Place on a baking sheet and bake in a very hot oven, 450 degrees, about 15 minutes or until brown.

14 biscuits.

Source: *Florida's Favorite Recipes for Citrus Fruits. A compilation of recipes which won top honors in county contests jointly sponsored by the Florida Agricultural Extension Service, home demonstration work, and the Florida Chain Store Council as a feature of Florida's "Eat More Citrus Month," February, 1954.* Lakeland, FL: Florida Citrus Commission, 1954.

Grapefruit Tea Biscuit

3 cups sifted plain flour
1 teaspoon salt
3 teaspoons sugar
½ teaspoon soda
3 teaspoons baking powder
¾ cup shortening
¾ cup strained grapefruit juice
¼ cup evaporated milk, undiluted

Sift flour, salt, sugar, soda, and baking powder together. Cub or rub in shortening until well blended. Mix grapefruit juice and milk. Add to dry ingredients, using just enough to make dough that is soft but not sticky. Turn dough onto a lightly floured board and knead a few strokes. Roll or pat to ⅛ inch thickness. Cut into small biscuits. Place on a baking sheet. Bake in a very hot oven, 475 degrees, 15 to 20 minutes. Serve hot with butter and orange marmalade.

24 biscuits.

Source: *Florida's Favorite Recipes for Citrus Fruits. A compilation of recipes which won top honors in county contests jointly sponsored by the Florida Agricultural Extension Service, home demonstration work, and the Florida Chain Store Council as a feature of Florida's "Eat More Citrus Month," February, 1954.* Lakeland, FL: Florida Citrus Commission, 1954.

Mango Nut Bread

½ cup butter or vegetable shortening
¾ cup sugar
2 eggs
⅔ cup raw mango, cut fine
2 cups sifted flour
1 teaspoon of soda
1 tablespoon of lime juice
¼ teaspoon salt
½ cup chopped nuts

Cream shortening and sugar. Add eggs. Stir in dry ingredients, mango, and lime juice. Mix all together. Add chopped nuts. Bake in a loaf pan at 375 degrees for 1 hour. Do not cut until the second day.

Source: *Florida Fruit and Vegetable Recipes.* Tallahassee, FL: Florida Department of Agriculture, no date.

Orange Banana Nut Bread

2½ cups sifted all-purpose flour
4 teaspoon baking powder
¾ teaspoon salt
¾ cup chopped Brazil nuts
1½ cups mixed candied fruits
⅓ cup raisins
½ cup shortening
¾ cup sugar
3 eggs
½ cup mashed banana
½ cup orange juice

Sift together flour, baking powder and salt. Stir in chopped nuts, candied fruits and raisins. Cream shortening. Add sugar and beat until light and fluffy. Add eggs, one at a time, beating after each addition. Combine mashed banana and orange juice; add to creamed mixture alternately with flour mixture, beginning and ending with dry ingredients. Turn into a waxed paper lined and greased 9 × 5 × 3 inch loaf pan. Bake in moderate oven, 350 degrees, 1 hour. Cool 20 to 30 minutes before turning out on cake rack.

1 loaf.

Source: *Florida Fruit and Vegetable Recipes.* Tallahassee, FL: Florida Department of Agriculture, no date.

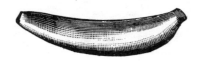

Banana tree showing bud and fruit in Florida. Asheville: Asheville Post Card Co., no date. Florida Postcard Collection. Archives and Special Collections, University of Miami Library.

Orange French Toast

1 egg
¼ cup orange juice
¼ cup granulated sugar
1½ teaspoons grated orange rind
3 slices bread
Butter or margarine
2 oranges, sliced or sectioned
Powdered sugar

Beat egg. Add orange and lemon juice and beat again. Add sugar and grated orange rind; mix thoroughly. Cut slices of bread in half or in any desired shape. Dip in egg mixture. Fry in butter or margarine until golden brown. Place orange slices or sections on each slice of toast. Sprinkle with powdered sugar. Serve immediately.

3 servings.

Source: *Florida's Favorite Recipes for Citrus Fruits. A compilation of recipes which won top honors in county contests jointly sponsored by the Florida Agricultural Extension Service, home demonstration work, and the Florida Chain Store Council as a feature of Florida's "Eat More Citrus Month," February, 1954.* Lakeland, FL: Florida Citrus Commission, 1954.

Orange Fritters

2 medium sized oranges, peeled, sliced ¼-inch thick and sprinkled
    with sugar
1 egg, beaten well
¼ cup milk
½ tablespoon melted butter
½ cup sifted flour
½ teaspoon baking powder
1 teaspoon sugar
¼ teaspoon salt

Mix beaten egg, milk, and melted butter. Sift flour, baking powder, sugar, and salt together. Stir into liquid. Dip orange slices in batter. Deep fry. Serve with Orange Syrup, page 53.

4 servings.

Source: *Florida's Favorite Recipes for Citrus Fruits. A compilation of recipes which won top honors in county contests jointly sponsored by the Florida Agricultural Extension Service, home demonstration work, and the Florida Chain Store Council as a feature of Florida's "Eat More Citrus Month," February, 1954.* Lakeland, FL: Florida Citrus Commission, 1954.

Orange Juice Gems

¼ cup butter or margarine
½ cup sugar
1 egg
1 tablespoon grated orange rind
½ cup chopped pecans
1¼ cups sifted cake flour
¼ teaspoon salt
1 teaspoon baking powder
¼ teaspoon baking soda
½ cup orange juice

Cream butter, add sugar gradually, blending thoroughly after each addition. Beat in egg. Stir in orange rind and pecans. Sift together flour, salt, baking powder and soda. Add dry ingredients alternately with orange juice, mixing well but quickly. Fill greased 2-inch muffin pans ⅔ full. Bake in moderate oven (375 degrees) 20 to 25 minutes. Remove from pan; cool. Insert fork into cupcake and dip in Orange Syrup, strike fork against edge of pan to allow excess syrup to drop off. Place on rack to cool.

Orange Syrup

½ cup orange juice
1 cup sugar
1 tablespoon grated orange rind

Combine orange juice, sugar and rind in small saucepan; stir over low heat until sugar is dissolved. Increase heat and boil rapidly for 5 minutes or until 230 degree temperature is reached on the candy thermometer.

About 22 gems.

Source: *Florida Citrus Fare.* Lakeland, FL: Florida Citrus Commission, no date.

Orange Muffins

½ cup coarsely grated orange rind
½ cup sugar
¼ cup water
4 tablespoons melted shortening
1 cup orange juice
1 egg, well-beaten
2 cups sifted flour
2 teaspoons baking powder
½ teaspoon salt
¼ teaspoon soda
4 tablespoons sugar

Combine sugar, water, and rind in a saucepan. Cook slowly for five minutes, stirring constantly. Remove from heat; add shortening; stir until melted. Add orange juice and beaten egg. Sift flour, baking powder, salt, soda, and sugar together. Add orange mixture; stir just enough to moisten ingredients. Batter should be lumpy. Fill greased muffin pans ⅔ full, handling the batter as little as possible. Bake in a hot oven, 425 degrees, 20 to 25 minutes. Serve while hot with orange marmalade.

16 muffins.

Source: *Florida's Favorite Recipes for Citrus Fruits. A compilation of recipes which won top honors in county contests jointly sponsored by the Florida Agricultural Extension Service, home demonstration work, and the Florida Chain Store Council as a feature of Florida's "Eat More Citrus Month," February, 1954.* Lakeland, FL: Florida Citrus Commission, 1954.

Orange Pecan Bird Nests

Topping

1 cup orange juice
1 cup brown sugar
1 cup dark corn syrup
3 eggs, slightly beaten
¼ teaspoon salt
1 tablespoon grated orange rind
¼ teaspoon nutmeg
¼ teaspoon ginger
¼ teaspoon cinnamon
1 cup pecan halves
1 orange sliced in half circles

Mix all ingredients together in a bowl. Set aside.

Bird Nests

10 thin biscuits or 1 can oven-ready biscuits
½ cup brown sugar (1 teaspoon for each nest)
2 cups drained orange sections (about 5 oranges)
10 pats or teaspoons of butter (1 for each nest)
40 pecan halves (2 for each nest)

Roll each biscuit with rolling pin between 2 sheets of waxed paper to about a circle 4 inches across. Sprinkle with brown sugar; then lay about 4 orange sections in center; top with pat of butter and 2 pecans. Dampen edges of circle and pinch together to make bird nests. Place these in a greased 2-inch deep pie pan. Remove orange half-circles from topping. Pour topping over bird nests. Decorate with orange slices to make scalloped effect around outside edge. Bake in a moderate oven, 375 degrees, about 1 hour.

10 servings.

Source: *Florida's Favorite Recipes for Citrus Fruits. A compilation of recipes which won top honors in county contests jointly sponsored by the Florida Agricultural Extension Service, home demonstration work, and the Florida Chain Store Council as a feature of Florida's "Eat More Citrus Month," February, 1954.* Lakeland, FL: Florida Citrus Commission, 1954.

Pancake Stacks & Florida Orange Sauce

1¼ cups sifted all-purpose flour
2½ teaspoons baking powder
¾ teaspoon salt
3 tablespoons sugar
1 egg, slightly beaten
¼ cup milk
¾ cup orange juice
3 tablespoons melted butter or margarine
1 to 2 cups cottage cheese

Sift together dry ingredients. Combine slightly beaten egg, milk, orange juice, and butter. Stir into dry ingredients. To make 4 large pancakes, bake on hot griddle, one at a time, using ⅔ cup batter for each pancake. Stack pancakes, spreading ⅓ cup cottage cheese between each. To serve, cut into wedges; spoon Florida Orange Sauce over top.

Florida Orange Sauce

Mix together 1 tablespoon cornstarch, ½ cup sugar, and ¼ teaspoon salt in a saucepan. Blend in one cup orange juice and add 2 teaspoons grated orange rind. Cook over medium heat until mixture comes to a boil, stirring constantly. Add 1 tablespoon butter or margarine and one orange, sectioned; heat. Yields about 1¼ cups.

4 to 6 servings.

Source: *Florida Fruit and Vegetable Recipes.* Tallahassee, FL: Florida Department of Agriculture, no date.

Pineapple Luncheon Sandwiches

1 cup finely diced cooked ham
1 cup crushed canned pineapple, drained
2 tablespoons milk or water
1 tablespoon prepared mustard
2 tablespoons pineapple juice
1 beaten egg

Mix first four ingredients together well and spread between slices of buttered bread. Dip each side of the prepared sandwiches in the beaten egg which has been combined with milk; saute until golden brown on both sides. Serve at once.

Source: *Florida's Favorite Foods. Fruits and Vegetables in the Family Menu.* Bulletin No. 46, Tallahassee, FL: Florida Department of Agriculture, 1959.

Sandwich Spread

Thin peanut butter or cream cheese with orange juice; add rind.

Source: *Florida Citrus Fare.* Lakeland, FL: Florida Citrus Commission, no date.

Our favorite seat in Bayfront Park on Biscayne Bay, Miami, 1930. Floyd and Marion Rinhart Collection. Archives and Special Collections, University of Miami Library.

Temple Orange Tea Bread

2 cups all-purpose flour
1½ teaspoons baking powder
1 teaspoon baking soda
½ teaspoon salt
⅔ cup nonfat plain yogurt
⅔ cup sugar
2 large eggs (egg substitute optional)
3 tablespoons melted unsalted butter or margarine
1 tablespoon grated orange zest

Syrup

½ cup Florida Temple orange juice
¼ cup sugar

Preheat oven to 350 degrees. Butter an 8½ × 4½ × 2⅝ nonstick loaf pan. Sift flour, baking powder, baking soda, and salt into a bowl. In a separate bowl, whisk together yogurt, sugar, eggs, butter, and orange zest. Add liquid ingredients to dry ingredients, and stir mixture until well combined. Transfer batter to loaf pan, smoothing top, and bake in oven for 45–50 minutes, or until skewer inserted in the middle comes out clean.

While the bread is baking, combine orange juice and sugar in a saucepan. Bring mixture to a boil over moderate heat while stirring, and simmer for 1 minute. Keep syrup warm.

Make holes in top of bread with a thin wooden skewer and brush top with syrup. Let stand in pan for 10 minutes, then invert onto rack. Poke holes in bottom and sides of bread with skewer, and brush with remaining syrup. Let bread cool standing upright, and wrap in plastic and foil overnight.

Makes 1 loaf = 17 slices.

Source: *Florida Citrus Cooking: Recipes from the Sunshine State.* Tallahassee, FL: Florida Department of Citrus, 1994.

Trudy Muffins

3 cups sifted flour
3 teaspoons baking powder
1 teaspoon salt
¼ cup cranberries, quartered
½ cup shortening
½ cup sugar
2 eggs
1 cup orange juice
1 cup orange pulp

Sift together flour, salt, and baking powder. Cream shortening and sugar. Add orange juice, orange pulp, and cranberries. Add to the dry ingredients all at once, stirring only enough to moisten. Fill greased muffin pans ⅔ full. Bake in a hot oven, 400 degrees, 25 to 30 minutes or until brown.

24 medium-sized muffins.

Source: *Florida's Favorite Recipes for Citrus Fruits. A compilation of recipes which won top honors in county contests jointly sponsored by the Florida Agricultural Extension Service, home demonstration work, and the Florida Chain Store Council as a feature of Florida's "Eat More Citrus Month," February, 1954.* Lakeland, FL: Florida Citrus Commission, 1954.

Whole Wheat French Toast with Florida Orange Slices

1 large egg
2 large egg whites
1 tablespoon low-fat milk
1 teaspoon grated orange zest
½ teaspoon vanilla extract
⅛ teaspoon ground cinnamon
1 tablespoon vegetable oil
4 slices whole wheat toast
Florida orange slices

In a shallow bowl, beat egg, egg whites, milk, orange zest, vanilla extract and cinnamon until blended. In a large nonstick skillet, heat oil over medium heat. Dip bread in egg mixture and add to skillet. Cook, turning once, until browned on both sides, 3–4 minutes per side. Serve hot with Florida Orange Slices.

Source: *Florida Citrus Cooking: Recipes from the Sunshine State.* Tallahassee, FL: Florida Department of Citrus, 1994.

Florida Orange Slices

2 seedless oranges, peeled (white pith removed), halved and sliced into rounds
2 teaspoons sugar
½ teaspoon vanilla extract

In a small bowl, combine Florida orange slices, sugar and vanilla extract, tossing to coat. Let stand 1 hour for flavors to blend.

Makes 4 servings.

Source: *Florida Citrus Cooking: Recipes from the Sunshine State.* Tallahassee, FL: Florida Department of Citrus, 1994.

Salads

Appetizer Salad in Grapefruit Baskets

Cut a grapefruit in half and make a four-section handled basket from each half in the following manner: Insert two toothpicks near cut edge opposite each other. From ¾ inch on each side of toothpick, cut through skin around the grapefruit ¼ inch from top of cut surface. Remove pulp from this cup part so that the two strips of peel can be tied together to form basket handle.

With a curved grapefruit knife, remove the pulp, leaving four of the white membrane divisions as partitions to form equal sized sections. Place a different salad or appetizer in each of the four sections. Tuna fish, celery, cucumber and a tiny bit of green pepper mixed with mayonnaise could be used for one; radish roses in another; celery curls or olives, green and ripe, in a third. In fourth section place diced grapefruit pulp and avocado which has been marinated with French dressing. Serve on salad plate as first course of a luncheon or dinner. Garnish top of partitions and center with mayonnaise forced through pastry bag.

Source: *Florida Fruits and Vegetables in the Family Menu.* Bulletin No. 46, New Series, Tallahassee, FL: Florida Department of Agriculture, 1956.

Avocado Salad

Cut a peeled avocado into rather thin slices crosswise, then cut each slice again once or twice the other way. Arrange on crisp leaves of lettuce alternately with segments of orange and grapefruit from which all the skin has been removed. Garnish with strips of pimento and serve with French dressing made with lemon juice, and only a little oil.

Source: *Florida Fruits and Vegetables in the Family Menu.* Bulletin No. 46, New Series, Tallahassee, FL: Florida Department of Agriculture, 1956.

A Seminole Indian mother and children preparing dinner, 1930. Floyd and Marion Rinhart Collection. Archives and Special Collections, University of Miami Library.

Banana Salads

Sprinkle the peeled fruit with lemon or lime juice. Roll in crushed peanuts. Serve on lettuce. Garnish with strawberries (with stems).

Marinate banana in lemon or sour orange juice, roll in crushed pecans, serve with ripe strawberries, fruit dressing.

Make a banana boat. Combine pulp with halved strawberries and fill the boat. Use a slightly sweetened lemon dressing. Serve the banana on strawberry leaves. Serve with toasted cheese crackers and Russian tea as a luncheon.

Source: *Florida Fruits and Vegetables in the Family Menu.* Bulletin No. 46, New Series, Tallahassee, FL: Florida Department of Agriculture, 1956.

Caugin Salad

Scoop all meat from bright, clear-skinned grapefruit halves (described in Appetizer Salad in Grapefruit Baskets). Scallop the edges. Dice avocado, orange, and grapefruit. Pile into grapefruit baskets. Sprinkle top with a little finely chopped canton ginger and green pepper. Place on pale glass plate, garnish with watercress. Serve with mayonnaise flavored with a little minced ginger and cognac.

Source: *Florida Fruits and Vegetables in the Family Menu.* Bulletin No. 46, New Series, Tallahassee, FL: Florida Department of Agriculture, 1956.

Citrus Salads

Florida Fruit Salad: Arrange grapefruit sections on salad greens with melon balls and berries or cherries. Garnish with watercress. Serve with French dressing.

Sarasota Salad: Mold tomato aspic in individual ring molds. Unmold and fill center with grapefruit sections. Serve with mayonnaise.

Southern Salad: Arrange grapefruit sections on salad greens. Add spoonful of cottage cheese to which onion juice or chopped chives have been added. Serve with French dressing.

Sunshine Special: Alternate orange and grapefruit sections on salad greens. Pile small grapes at side. Garnish with mint. Serve with French dressing made with grapefruit juice.

Tossed Salad: Break chilled crisp salad greens (watercress, escarole, romaine, endive, chicory) into small pieces in large salad bowl. Arrange over greens 1½ cups grapefruit sections and ½ medium-sized avocado cut in wedges. Add French dressing and toss ingredients together lightly. Variations: Add ½ cup diced celery and 1 cup flaked crabmeat, shrimp, diced lobster, diced chicken or turkey, slivered ham.

Source: *Florida Citrus Fare.* Lakeland, FL: Florida Citrus Commission, no date.

Citus Slimmer Salad

¾ **cup uncreamed cottage cheese**
1 tablespoon frozen orange juice concentrate, thawed, undiluted
1 tablespoon chopped green pepper
¼ **teaspoon salt**
Lettuce
1 cup orange and grapefruit sections

Combine cottage cheese with undiluted concentrate, green pepper, and salt. Arrange lettuce, cottage cheese, and citrus sections on salad plate.

1 serving.

Source: *Care and Handling of Florida Citrus.* 13-23-CHB-7764, Lakeland, FL: Florida Department of Citrus, 1982.

Dazzling Strawberry 'n' Avocado Salad

1 8-ounce package of cream cheese, softened
¼ **cup milk**
¾ **teaspoon ginger**
1 6-ounce can frozen limeade concentrate, thawed
2 cups avocados, cut into bite-size chunks
2 cups strawberry halves
Romaine or other lettuce leaves

In small bowl, with electric mixer at medium speed, beat cheese, milk, ginger and 3 tablespoons limeade concentrate until smooth. Set aside. In large bowl, toss avocado and strawberries with remaining limeade. With slotted spoon, transfer avocado-strawberry mixture to lettuce-lined plates or fruit cups.

6 servings.

Source: *Florida Recipes.* Tallahassee, FL: Florida Department of Agriculture and Consumer Services, no date.

Flamingo Salad

Guavas
Nuts
Lettuce
Cottage Cheese
Green Peppers
Surinam Cherries

On a bed of lettuce, endive, or thinly sliced Chinese cabbage, place a chain of rose-colored guava rings. In center of rings, place a mound of cottage cheese and chopped nuts. Decorate the top of the cheese mixture with julienned green peppers and with pieces of guava in form of small flower and place Surinam cherry in center. Carissa also makes a pretty garnish. Salmon-colored or yellow guavas may be used instead of the red, with kumquats used as the garnish.

Source: *Growing and Preparing Guavas.* Bulletin No. 74, Tallahassee, FL: Florida Department of Agriculture, 1957.

Florida King Crab

On one of the dessert pedestals or in a bowl, arrange a base of shredded iceberg lettuce. Arrange three panels of grapefruit sections, king crab legs, and marinated asparagus. Garnish with ripe olives and parsley.

Source: *Chilled Florida Citrus Sections for Around the Year Profit.* CCS-1, Lakeland, FL: Florida Citrus Commission, no date.

Florida Salad

1 grapefruit
French Dressing
1 Spanish onion
Lettuce leaves

Buy solid grapefruits. Peel and slice in round slices. Slice onions. Lay slices of grapefruit on bed of lettuce, and lay slice of onion and strip of pimento on grapefruit. Pour over it the French dressing.

Source: *Florida Fruits and Vegetables in the Family Menu.* Bulletin No. 46, New Series, Tallahassee, FL: Florida Department of Agriculture, 1956.

Florida Sunshine Salad

Leaf or romaine lettuce
1 cup low-fat cottage cheese
1 orange, peeled, cut in wheels
½ pink grapefruit, peeled, cut in wheels
1 sprig fresh mint
1 kiwi fruit, peeled and sliced
1 white grapefruit, peeled and sectioned
3-4 strawberries, sliced
2 tablespoons coarsely chopped nuts
Red or green grapes (optional)

Wash and dry lettuce, make into a bed on a round dinner plate. Arrange in a shingled pattern: grapefruit segments, kiwi slices, orange wheels and grapefruit wheels. Top with scoop of cottage cheese. Garnish with strawberries, grapes, nuts, and fresh mint.

Source: *Florida Citrus Sampler.* Lakeland, FL: Florida Department of Citrus, no date.

French Dressing No. 1

3 tablespoons lemon juice
6 tablespoons salad oil
¼ teaspoon paprika
¼ teaspoon salt

Stir or shake thoroughly before serving. Use a tightly closed jar for mixing large amounts. Keep in refrigerator until ready to use.

Makes about ½ cup.

Source: *Florida Fruits and Vegetables in the Family Menu.* Bulletin No. 46, New Series, Tallahassee, FL: Florida Department of Agriculture, 1956.

French Dressing No. 2

To ½ cup French Dressing, add 2 tablespoons strained honey. Serve on fruit salads.

Makes about ½ cup.

Source: *Florida Fruits and Vegetables in the Family Menu.* Bulletin No. 46, New Series, Tallahassee. FL: Florida Department of Agriculture, 1956.

French Dressing No. 3

3 tablespoons lemon juice
3 tablespoons orange juice
4 tablespoons oil
¼ teaspoon salt
½ teaspoon sugar or honey

Mix all ingredients thoroughly.

Makes about ½ cup.

Source: *Florida Fruits and Vegetables in the Family Menu.* Bulletin No. 46, New Series, Tallahassee, FL: Florida Department of Agriculture, 1956.

French Dressing No. 4

3 quarts grapefruit juice (unsweetened, canned or reconstituted
    frozen juice)
½ cup cornstarch
1½ cups salad oil
2½ tablespoons salt
6 tablespoons sugar
1 tablespoons paprika
1 tablespoon dry mustard
2 teaspoons Tabasco
3 cups catsup
4 cloves garlic, optional

Blend 3 cups of the grapefruit juice and cornstarch in saucepan. Cook over low heat stirring constantly until thickened. Remove from heat; stir in remaining grapefruit juice. Combine remaining ingredients except garlic. Add grapefruit mixture and beat until blended. Add garlic. Shake or stir before serving. Store covered in refrigerator.

1 gallon.

Source: *Chilled Florida Citrus Sections For Around the Year Profit.* CCS-1, Lakeland, FL: Florida Citrus Commission, no date.

Grapefruit and Cheese Salads

Salad No. 1

Peel a grapefruit, separate the sections, skin them and keep them whole. Slice and peel a small ripe pineapple, cut into little cubes and arrange these on crisp lettuce leaves.

Surround with grapefruit sections, petal fashion. Place a piece of Roquefort, gruyere, brie, or cream cheese on the pineapple. Garnish with a strip of pimento. Serve with French dressing.

Salad No. 2

Peel two grapefruit, cutting away the white skin. Remove pulp, keeping each section whole. Arrange five sections of the fruit like petals of a daisy on leaves of crisp romaine or lettuce. Place a teaspoon of grated American cheese around the inner points of the fruit sections to carry out the idea of the flower. Serve with French dressing.

Salad No. 3

Grapefruit
French dressing
Roquefort cheese
Green pepper, minced or in thin strips
Watercress

Peel grapefruit and slice thinly across; cut in half again cross wise, rejecting all seeds; allow 2 slices for portion. Arrange on cress-covered plates.

Pour dressing over, in which Roquefort cheese has been smoothly mashed. Garnish with minced pepper or pepper strips.

Serves 6.

Source: *Florida Fruits and Vegetables in the Family Menu.* Bulletin No. 46, New Series, Tallahassee, FL: Florida Department of Agriculture, 1956.

Grapefruit Box Salad

1 cup diced grapefruit pulp
½ cup seeded white cherries
½ cup seeded red cherries
½ cup diced marshmallows
½ cup nut meats
Saltines

Mix ingredients. Arrange on lettuce-covered plates. Place 4 saltines like a box around salad, and tie in shape with narrow ribbon to match preferred color scheme.

Source: *Florida Fruits and Vegetables in the Family Menu.* Bulletin No. 46, New Series, Tallahassee, FL: Florida Department of Agriculture, 1956.

Grapefruit Salad Dressing

1 cup salad oil
Dash of pepper
⅓ cup grapefruit juice
¾ teaspoon salt
½ teaspoon sugar

Mix all ingredients and shake in a covered bottle until thick.

Source: *Florida Fruits and Vegetables in the Family Menu.* Bulletin No. 46, New Series, Tallahassee, FL: Florida Department of Agriculture, 1956.

Grapefruit Salmon Salad

½ cup diced apple
2 cups grapefruit
Desired amount of watercress
½ cup diced celery
1 cup smoked salmon

Season well and mix with French dressing or mayonnaise.

Source: *Florida's Favorite Foods. Fruits and Vegetables in the Family Menu.* Bulletin No. 46, Tallahassee, FL: Florida Department of Agriculture, 1959.

Grapefruit Seafood Salad

¼ cup salad oil

2 large cloves garlic, minced

2 cups green beans, cut in 1-inch pieces

1 pound scallops

2 cups grapefruit sections, grapefruit juice, drained from sections, approximately ⅓ cup

3 tablespoons vinegar

¾ teaspoon crushed fennel seeds

¼ teaspoon salt

½ cup sliced, pitted black olives

In medium skillet, heat oil; cook garlic until golden. Add green beans; stir-fry 2 to 3 minutes until crisp-tender. Remove with slotted spoon to large bowl. In same skillet, stir-fry scallops 2 to 3 minutes until done. Remove with slotted spoon and add to green beans. Add grapefruit juice to skillet. Stir in vinegar, fennel seeds, and salt. Boil mixture, uncovered, until reduced to ⅓ cup. Return beans and scallops to skillet. Add grapefruit sections and olives; toss lightly. Serve immediately.

4 servings.

Source: *Willard Scott: My Favorite Florida Citrus Recipes.* Lakeland, FL: Florida Department of Citrus, no date.

Grapefruit Shrimp Salad

1 cup grapefruit sections, cut in pieces
⅓ cup cucumber, diced
⅓ cup mayonnaise
1 cup boiled shrimp, cut in pieces
¾ cup celery, diced
Lettuce, pimiento

Add ingredients in order given. Chill in refrigerator and serve on crisp lettuce. Garnish with small pimiento strips.

Serves 6.

Source: *Florida Fruits and Vegetables in the Family Menu.* Bulletin No. 46, New Series, Tallahassee. FL: Florida Department of Agriculture, 1956.

Guacamole

1 medium avocado
2 3-ounce packages cream cheese
2 teaspoons lime juice
¼ teaspoon Tabasco
¼ teaspoon salt
½ teaspoon Worcestershire sauce

Cut avocados in half lengthwise; remove pit. Peel skin from halves; mash pulp. Add remaining ingredients; beat with electric beater until smooth. Use as dip for potato chips or crisp crackers.

1½ cups.

Source: *Florida's Favorite Foods. Fruits and Vegetables in the Family Menu.* Bulletin No. 46, Tallahassee, FL: Florida Department of Agriculture, 1959.

Guava Salads

(1) Marinate guava cups in lemon juice. Fill with grated coconut and orange. Serve with mayonnaise in a lettuce nest.

(2) Stuff guava cups with strawberries or with congealed guava pulp and pecans. Use cream dressing (sweetened). (Marinate cup with lemon to prevent darkening.)

(3) Guava, celery, and cheese.

(4) Guava, pineapple, pecans, crystallized fig.

(5) Halves of guava, center filled with cheese, topped with carissa (Natal-plum) or Surinam cherry.

Source: *Florida's Favorite Foods. Fruits and Vegetables in the Family Menu.* Bulletin No. 46, Tallahassee, FL: Florida Department of Agriculture, 1959.

Buying oranges and grapefruit at the grove, Homestead, FL, 1932. Floyd and Marion Rinhart Collection. Archives and Special Collections, University of Miami Library.

Mixed Citrus Compote with Florida Orange-Lime Syrup

1 cup sugar
½ cup Florida orange juice
2 tablespoons fresh lime juice
1 tablespoon grated orange zest
2 teaspoons grated lime zest
4 seedless oranges, peeled (white pith removed) and sectioned
2 Florida tangerines, seeded, peeled (white pith removed) and
   sectioned
2 red or pink grapefruit, peeled (white pith removed) and sectioned
2 limes, peeled (white pith removed) and sectioned

In a small saucepan, heat sugar, orange juice, and lime juice over medium heat until sugar dissolves. Remove from heat; add orange zest and lime zest, and cool. In a medium bowl, combine the fruit. Add syrup, stirring gently to combine. Chill at least 1 hour before serving.

Makes 8 servings.

Source: *Florida Citrus Cooking: Recipes from the Sunshine State.* Tallahassee, FL: Florida Department of Citrus, 1994.

Molded Citrus Dessert or Salad

1 envelope unflavored gelatin
1¾ cups canned tangerine, grapefruit, orange or blended juice
2 tablespoons sugar (for salad)
4 tablespoons sugar (for dessert)
⅛ teaspoon salt
1½ cups canned grapefruit sections, well drained

Soften gelatin in ½ cup citrus juice. Heat remaining 1¼ cups juice; add gelatin, sugar and salt; stir until dissolved. Chill until slightly thickened. Fold in grapefruit sections. Chill in individual molds until firm. Unmold on crisp greens; serve with salad dressing, or as dessert with whipped cream.

6 servings.

Source: *Florida Citrus Fare.* Lakeland, FL: Florida Citrus Commission, no date.

A large grove of young orange trees, 1928. Floyd and Marion Rinhart Collection. Archives and Special Collections, University of Miami Library.

Orange Pecan Slaw

1 small head green or red cabbage, shredded (about 12 cups), or red
    and green cabbage mixed
1 cup chopped pecans
4 oranges, peeled and diced
¾ cup bottled slaw dressing
1 tablespoon lemon juice
1 tablespoon honey
½ teaspoon salt (optional)

In large mixing bowl, combine cabbage, pecans and orange pieces. In small bowl or jar, combine slaw dressing, lemon juice, honey and salt; stir or shake to blend well. Pour dressing over slaw. Toss lightly. Cover. Chill 1 hour.

6–8 servings.

Source: *Willard Scott: My Favorite Florida Citrus Recipes.* Lakeland, FL: Florida Department of Citrus, no date.

Palm Beach Chicken Salad

½ cup chicken broth

2 whole chicken breasts, boned and skinned

1½ cups uncooked pasta

1 cup peas, cooked, drained

½ cup pimiento, diced

2 cups grapefruit sections, grapefruit juice, drained from sections, approximately ⅓ cup

¼ cup salad oil

2 tablespoons wine vinegar

1 large clove garlic, minced

½ teaspoon ground cumin

½ teaspoon salt

⅛ teaspoon white pepper

In medium skillet, bring broth to a boil. Arrange chicken breasts in single layer in pan; return broth to boiling. Cover. Cook about 10 minutes, until chicken is cooked through. Drain. In large bowl, combine chicken, pasta, peas, pimiento, grapefruit sections, and juice. In a small bowl or jar, combine oil, vinegar, garlic, cumin, salt, and pepper; mix well. Pour dressing over chicken mixture; toss lightly. Serve warm.

4 servings.

Source: *Willard Scott: My Favorite Florida Citrus Recipes.* Lakeland, FL: Florida Department of Citrus, no date.

Papaya Citrus Salad

2 cups ripe papaya peeled and cut in 1-inch slices
1 cup grapefruit sections, canned or fresh
1 green pepper cut small
2 young onions, cut fine
1 cup orange sections
4 stalks celery, cut fine
½ cup carrots, cut fine
½ cup thinly sliced kumquats
French dressing
Crisp lettuce

Blend all ingredients together and place on cold, crisp lettuce. Season with French dressing and serve with crisp crackers or cheese wafers.

Source: *The Papaya. A Fruit Suitable for South Florida.* Bulletin No. 90, New Series, Tallahassee, FL: Florida Department of Agriculture, 1939.

Papaya Salad

4 cups ripe papaya cut in cubes
6 teaspoons finely chopped onion
1 teaspoon salt
¾ cup salad dressing or mayonnaise well seasoned
1 cup finely chopped celery

Cut papaya into cubes, add the chopped onion and celery. Chill, serve on lettuce leaves and garnish with mayonnaise.

Source: *The Papaya. A Fruit Suitable for South Florida.* Bulletin No. 90, New Series, Tallahassee, FL: Florida Department of Agriculture, 1939.

Persimmons and Grapefruit Salad

Select soft, transparent persimmons. Peel by beginning at the blossom end and work toward the stem so the fruit may hold its shape. Cut into sections the size of grapefruit sections. If not using canned grapefruit sections, prepare the fresh fruit by cutting away all skin and membrane from each section of the "heart" using a very sharp knife.

On a salad plate, arrange a bed of shredded lettuce, endive, or cabbage, and on it alternate the persimmon and grapefruit sections around a central point to make the salad resemble a flower, using a spoonful of mayonnaise in the center to complete the flower idea. Serve with either a French dressing or a fruit mayonnaise.

Source: *Florida Fruits and Vegetables in the Family Menu.* Bulletin No. 46, New Series, Tallahassee, FL: Florida Department of Agriculture, 1956.

Romaine Delight

On romaine lettuce, arrange orange sections and red apple slices alternately. Pipe on a frill of cream cheese and sprinkle with chopped walnuts. Decorate with more orange sections.

Source: *Chilled Florida Citrus Sections for Around the Year Profit.* CCS-1, Lakeland, FL: Florida Citrus Commission, no date.

Sea Breeze

Combine grapefruit sections and chilled whole shrimp. Refrigerate 1 hour to develop flavor. Line shell-shaped servers with lettuce. Fill with grapefruit-shrimp mixture. Garnish with crisp celery stalk and lime wedge.

Source: *Chilled Florida Citrus Sections for Around the Year Profit.* CCS-1, Lakeland, FL: Florida Citrus Commission, no date.

Shrimp Paradise Salad

¾ pound cooked, peeled, and cleaned shrimp, fresh or frozen
  or
3 cans (4½ or 5 ounces each) shrimp
1 pineapple
2 oranges
1 avocado
1 tablespoon orange juice

Thaw frozen shrimp or drain canned shrimp. Rinse canned shrimp with cold water. Chill. Cut pineapple in half lengthwise. Remove core and meat, reserving shell for serving. Dice pineapple. Peel and section oranges, reserving juice. Cut avocado in half lengthwise and remove seed. Peel and slice avocado. Sprinkle with orange juice to prevent discoloration. Combine pineapple, oranges, and avocado. Fill pineapple shells with fruit mixture. Arrange shrimp on top. Serve with Shrimp Paradise Salad Dressing.

Shrimp Paradise Salad Dressing

½ cup olive or salad oil
2 tablespoons lemon juice
2 tablespoons dry, white wine
1 teaspoon honey
¼ teaspoon paprika
½ teaspoon salt

Combine all ingredients and shake well. Chill. Makes approximately ¾ cup dressing.

Serves 6.

Source: *Florida Fish Recipes.* Fishery Market Development Series No. 1, Washington: U.S. Government Printing Office, 1966.

Sunshine Salad

1 grapefruit, sectioned
1 orange, sectioned
1 tangerine or tangelo, sectioned
1 avocado, sliced or cut in cubes
1 small onion, sliced very thinly and rings separated

Combine and top with Florida Dressing.

Florida Dressing

Juice of 1 lime
Juice of 1 lemon
1 teaspoon sugar, or more if desired
1 teaspoon salad oil
¼ teaspoon prepared mustard, if desired
⅛ teaspoon salt

Mix all ingredients. Shake vigorously. Pour over fruit salad. Toss lightly. Arrange fruit on lettuce.

Variation: For individual luncheon salads, cut avocado in halves or thirds. Place in lettuce cups. Place citrus and onion over the top.

Source: *Florida's Favorite Recipes for Citrus Fruits. A compilation of recipes which won top honors in county contests jointly sponsored by the Florida Agricultural Extension Service, home demonstration work, and the Florida Chain Store Council as a feature of Florida's "Eat More Citrus Month," February, 1954.* Lakeland, FL: Florida Citrus Commission, 1954.

Tangerine Slaw

Add halved tangerine sections to shredded cabbage, diced celery, and green pepper. Moisten with mayonnaise.

Source: *Florida Citrus Fare*. Lakeland, FL: Florida Citrus Commission, no date.

Tropical Salsa

3 grapefruit
2 medium oranges
1 medium mango (diced)
½ small red onion (peeled and diced)
1 small red pepper (julienne)
1 small yellow pepper (julienne)
1 large Anaheim chili pepper (julienne)
2 tablespoons cilantro (chopped)
¼ teaspoon salt
1 teaspoon olive oil

Peel and segment the grapefruit and oranges. Also squeeze the juice. Combine the cut grapefruit, oranges, mango, red onion, red pepper, yellow pepper, Anaheim chili, cilantro, salt, and olive oil. Toss carefully.

6 servings.

Source: *Taste the Tropics with Florida Grapefruit*. Lakeland, FL: Florida Department of Citrus, no date.

Twin Salute

On a platter, arrange a small chicken salad and garnish with toasted almond slivers. Add a second small salad of orange and grapefruit sections and cherries. Garnish with preserved kumquats.

Source: *Chilled Florida Citrus Sections For Around the Year Profit.* CCS-1, Lakeland, FL: Florida Citrus Commission, no date.

Soups, Stews, Sauces, Etc.

Basic 7 Sandwich

12 thin slices of bread
Soft butter
12 lettuce leaves
½ cup orange juice (1 medium orange)
(For a more piquant flavor, lemon juice may be substituted for one
    half the orange juice)
1 large banana, mashed
3 tablespoons grated cheese
3 tablespoons grated carrots
2 tablespoons grated or finely chopped pecans
3 tablespoons flaked tuna or other fish or meat

Lightly butter one side of each slice of sandwich bread. Mix all other ingredients well. Spread 6 slices of bread with the mixture, 3

6-1 Strawberry farm at Winter Garden, FL, 1928. Floyd and Marion Rinhart Collection. Archives and Special Collections, University of Miami Library.

tablespoons for each slice. Place a lettuce leaf and top with another slice of bread, buttered side down.

6 sandwiches.

Source: *Florida's Favorite Recipes for Citrus Fruits. A compilation of recipes which won top honors in county contests jointly sponsored by the Florida Agricultural Extension Service, home demonstration work, and the Florida Chain Store Council as a feature of Florida's "Eat More Citrus Month," February, 1954.* Lakeland, FL: Florida Citrus Commission, 1954.

Chilled Strawberry Soup

2 pints strawberries, hulled and washed
½ cup sugar
1 cup water
2 teaspoons lime juice, strained
¼ teaspoon lime peel
⅓ cup dry white wine
⅓ cup orange juice
1½ pints yogurt
¾ cup heavy whipping cream
Sugar to taste
Fresh mint sprigs
Whipped cream

Reserve 8 large perfect berries. Puree remaining berries in a blender or food processor, two cups at a time. Set aside. In a large saucepan over medium heat, simmer sugar, water, lime juice, lime peel, wine, and orange juice for 10 minutes. Let cool. Stir pureed berries into syrup and fold in yogurt and cream. Add sugar if desired. Cover and chill for 4 to 6 hours. Garnish individual servings with whole berries, mint sprigs, and whipped cream.

8 servings.

Source: *Serve Florida's Freshness.* Tallahassee, FL: Florida Department of Agriculture and Consumer Services, 1990.

Fluffy Lemon Sauce

2 tablespoons margarine or butter
2 tablespoons all-purpose flour
½ teaspoon salt
¼ teaspoon paprika
1¼ cups milk
½ cup mayonnaise or salad dressing
2 teaspoons lemon juice

Melt margarine in a 1-quart saucepan. Blend in flour, salt, and paprika. Gradually add milk; cook until thickened, stirring constantly. Stir in mayonnaise and lemon juice, blending thoroughly. Heat, but do not boil. Serve over warm poached or baked fish.

Makes approximately 1¾ cups sauce.

Source: *Florida Soups & Stews*. Tallahassee, FL: Florida Department of Natural Resources, no date.

Grapefruit Soup

1½ cups grapefruit juice
¼ cup peeled, grated beets
1 cup apple cider
1 teaspoon butter
Salt and white pepper to taste

Cook grapefruit juice and beets 10 minutes. Add apple cider, butter, salt and pepper. Heat.

4 servings.

Source: *Florida's Favorite Recipes for Citrus Fruits. A compilation of recipes which won top honors in county contests jointly sponsored by the Florida Agricultural Extension Service, home demonstration work, and the Florida Chain Store Council as a feature of Florida's "Eat More Citrus Month," February, 1954*. Lakeland, FL: Florida Citrus Commission, 1954.

Orange Spread

3 cups orange juice and pulp
1½ cups sugar
3 tablespoons cornstarch or flour
1 tablespoon butter

Cook orange juice and pulp, sugar, and cornstarch over low heat until thick, stirring to keep it from lumping. Remove from heat. Add butter.

Suggestions for serving: as a spread for hot breads, or as a filling between layers of cake, or as a pie filling.

Source: *Florida's Favorite Recipes for Citrus Fruits. A compilation of recipes which won top honors in county contests jointly sponsored by the Florida Agricultural Extension Service, home demonstration work, and the Florida Chain Store Council as a feature of Florida's "Eat More Citrus Month," February, 1954.* Lakeland, FL: Florida Citrus Commission, 1954.

Floating diner, ca. 1869. C. Seaver, Jr., photographer. Boston: Charles Pollock, 1869–1870. Floyd and Marion Rinhart Collection. Archives and Special Collections, University of Miami Library.

Entrees

Baked Spareribs with Orange Sauce

Quantity Serving

15-18 pounds ribs
1 gallon orange juice
1 quart catsup
1 pint cider vinegar
¼ ounce garlic
½ ounce salt
¼ ounce cayenne pepper
½ ounce Coleman's mustard

Family Serving

2½ to 3 pounds ribs
3 cups orange juice
¾ cup catsup
½ cup vinegar
Dash garlic
Dash salt
Dash cayenne pepper
Dash Coleman's mustard

Mix and blend well. Steam ribs until half done, cool off, dip in mixed sauce and barbecue on grill.

Source: *Famous Florida Chefs' Favorite Citrus Recipes.* Lakeland, FL: Florida Citrus Commission, no date.

Buttermilk Fried Mullet with Lemon Relish

2 pounds skinless mullet fillets or other skinless fish fillets, fresh or frozen
1 cup buttermilk
1 cup biscuit mix
2 teaspoons salt
Oil for deep frying
Lemon relish

Thaw fish if frozen. Cut fish into serving-size portions. Place fish in a single layer in a shallow dish. Pour buttermilk over fish and let stand for 30 minutes, turning once. Combine biscuit mix and salt. Remove fish from buttermilk and coat with biscuit mix. Place fish in a single layer in a fryer basket. Deep-fry in hot oil, 350 degrees, 3 to 5 minutes or until fish is brown and flakes easily when tested with a fork. Drain on absorbent paper. Serve with Lemon Relish.

Lemon Relish

½ cup sour cream
¼ cup crushed pineapple, drained
2 tablespoons diced, peeled lemon
2 tablespoons finely chopped green pepper
1 tablespoon finely chopped onion
1 tablespoon light brown sugar
1½ teaspoons grated lemon peel
¼ teaspoon dry mustard
¼ teaspoon celery salt
⅛ teaspoon ground cloves

Combine all ingredients; mix well. Chill. Makes approximately 1 cup relish.

6 servings.

Source: *Florida Mullet Recipes.* Tallahassee, FL: Florida Department of Natural Resources, no date.

Cherry Plaza Roast Duck

4 to 5 pound duck
2 teaspoons salt
¼ teaspoon pepper
1½ cups orange stuffing

Sprinkle duck with salt and pepper. Stuff and tie securely with wings and legs close to body. Sear in hot oven, with breast side up, 450 degrees, for 15 minutes. Add ½ pint of water and baste. Reduce heat to 350. Baste often. Cook about 45 minutes per pound.

Orange Stuffing

2 cups bread crumbs
½ cup water
2 tablespoons grated orange peel
2 cups orange pulp
1 cup sliced celery
1 egg beaten
¼ cup melted butter
½ teaspoon salt
Dash pepper
Dash poultry seasoning

Soften bread in water, add other ingredients, and mix thoroughly.

Source: *Famous Florida Chefs' Favorite Citrus Recipes*. Lakeland, FL: Florida Citrus Commission, no date.

Citrus Marinated Shrimp

1 cup frozen grapefruit juice concentrate, thawed
2 cloves garlic, minced
3 tablespoons chopped cilantro or parsley
2 teaspoons ketchup
1 tablespoon honey
¼ teaspoon red pepper flakes
½ teaspoon salt
1 pound medium shrimp, shelled and deveined
2 teaspoons cornstarch
1 cup long-grain white rice or pasta
1 tablespoon olive oil
1 large red pepper, slivered
2 stalks celery, sliced diagonally, ¼ inch thick
2 grapefruit, peeled and sectioned

In a medium bowl, combine grapefruit juice concentrate, garlic, cilantro or parsley, ketchup, honey, red pepper flakes and salt. Add the shrimp and stir. Allow to marinate 20 minutes, turning shrimp once. Drain the shrimp and reserve the marinade, combining it with cornstarch. Meanwhile, prepare rice or pasta according to package directions. In a large non-stick skillet, heat oil over medium-high heat. Add shrimp and saute 2 to 3 minutes or until shrimp begins to turn orange, just beginning to caramelize. Add red pepper, celery, and reserved marinade. Bring to a boil over high heat, stirring constantly until shrimp is just cooked through and sauce has thickened slightly. Add grapefruit sections and heat 30 seconds. Garnish with fresh sprigs of cilantro or parsley. Serve over rice or pasta.

4 servings.

Source: *Taste the Tropics with Florida Grapefruit.* Lakeland, FL: Florida Department of Citrus, no date.

Citrus Salmon Almondine

1 gallon water
3½ cups cider vinegar
3½ cups packed brown sugar
½ pound gingersnaps, crushed
¼ cup salt
⅓ cup lemon juice
8 bay leaves
12 lemons, peeled and sliced
6 grapefruit, sectioned
2 cups seedless green grapes
2 cups sliced almonds
½ cup light raisins
6 hot red peppers (optional)
12 oranges, sliced
20 8-ounce portions salmon fillets (or other boneless white fish)
4 large onions, sliced
12 sprigs parsley
Lettuce leaves

In a 4-inch pan, combine water, vinegar, brown sugar, gingersnap crumbs, salt, lemon juice, and bay leaves. Bring to a boil and stir until smooth. Add lemon slices, grapefruit sections, grapes, almonds, raisins and hot pepper; simmer 10 minutes. Add orange slices, fish, onion, and parsley. Cover and simmer over low heat 7 to 10 minutes, until fish is cooked. Remove from heat and allow entire pan to chill several hours or overnight. Remove fillets from broth. Serve chilled and garnished with fresh orange and grapefruit, if desired, and a parsley sprig.

20 servings.

Source: *Florida Citrus Sampler.* Lakeland, FL: Florida Department of Citrus, no date.

Citrus Stir-Fry

⅓ cup grapefruit juice
3 tablespoons soy sauce
3 tablespoons vegetable oil, divided
½ teaspoon ground ginger
1 pound boneless pork loin, cut into very thin strips
1 tablespoon cornstarch
¾ pound sea scallops, cut into thin slices
1 cup green onions or scallions, cut in 1-inch pieces
1 cup carrots, cut into thin strips
1 cup celery, sliced diagonally
2 grapefruit, peeled and sectioned
Hot, cooked rice
Green pepper, julienned (optional)

In a small bowl, combine grapefruit juice, soy sauce, 1 tablespoon oil, and ginger. Add pork strips; cover and let marinate 1 hour at room temperature. Drain pork. Reserve marinade. Combine marinade and cornstarch; set aside.

In a large skillet or wok, heat remaining 2 tablespoons oil over high heat. Add pork and stir-fry 2 to 3 minutes until browned. Add scallops and continue stir-frying another 2 minutes. Add reserved marinade mixture and green onions, continue stirring until sauce boils and thickens. Gently stir in grapefruit sections. Serve over hot rice. Garnish with green pepper, if desired.

6 servings.

Source: *Taste the Tropics with Florida Grapefruit.* Lakeland, FL: Florida Department of Citrus, no date.

Florida Glazed Chicken

5 cans (12 ounce each) frozen orange juice concentrate thawed,
   undiluted
1½ cups soy sauce
2 teaspoons pepper
1 tablespoon salt
4 garlic cloves, crushed
1½ cups slivered candied ginger
50 halves broiler/fryer chickens

Combine undiluted orange concentrate, soy sauce, pepper, salt, garlic, and ginger. Pour over chickens in shallow roasting pans. Let marinate in refrigerator about 3 hours or overnight, turning occasionally. Drain. Bake in 375 degree oven about 30 minutes on each side, or until done. Spoon any leftover marinade over chicken at serving time.

50 servings of one-half chicken.

Source: *Florida Citrus Sampler.* Lakeland, FL: Florida Department of Citrus, no date.

Florida Grapefruit Marinated Shrimp

1 cup frozen grapefruit juice concentrate, thawed
2 cloves garlic, minced
3 tablespoons chopped cilantro or parsley
2 teaspoons ketchup
1 tablespoon honey
¼ teaspoon red pepper flakes
½ teaspoon salt
1 pound medium shrimp, shelled and deveined
2 teaspoons cornstarch
1 cup long-grain white rice
1 tablespoon olive oil
1 large red pepper, slivered
2 stalks celery, sliced diagonally, ¼ inch thick
2 grapefruit, peeled and sectioned

In a medium bowl, combine grapefruit juice concentrate, garlic, cilantro or parsley, ketchup, honey, red pepper flakes, and salt. Add the shrimp, and stir. Allow to marinate 20 minutes, turning shrimp once. Drain the shrimp and reserve the marinade, combining it with cornstarch. Meanwhile, prepare rice according to package directions. In a large, nonstick skillet, heat oil over medium-high heat. Add shrimp and saute 2–3 minutes or until shrimp begins to turn orange, just beginning to caramelize. Add red pepper, celery, and reserved marinade. Bring to a boil over high heat, stirring constantly until shrimp is just cooked through and sauce has thickened slightly. Add grapefruit sections, and heat 30 seconds. Garnish with fresh sprigs of cilantro or parsley. Serve over rice.

4 servings.

Source: *Florida Citrus Cooking:* Recipes from the Sunshine State. Tallahassee, FL: Florida Department of Citrus, 1994.

Florida Grilled Yellowfin Tuna

2 pounds Florida yellowfin tuna steaks, fresh or frozen
¼ cup orange juice
¼ cup soy sauce
2 tablespoons ketchup
2 tablespoons vegetable oil
2 tablespoons chopped parsley
1 tablespoon lemon juice
1 clove garlic, finely chopped
½ teaspoon oregano
½ teaspoon pepper

Thaw steaks if frozen. Cut into serving-size portions and place in a single layer in a shallow baking dish. Combine remaining ingredients. Pour sauce over steaks and refrigerate 30 minutes, turning once. Remove fish, reserving sauce for basting. Place fish in well-greased,

Feeding peacocks at peacock farm, St.Petersburg 1935. Floyd and Marion Rinhart Collection. Archives and Special Collections, University of Miami Library.

hinged wire grills. Cook about 4 inches from moderately hot coals 5 to 6 minutes. Baste with sauce. Turn and cook for 4 to 5 minutes longer or until steak reaches 140 degrees, internally. Tuna should have a pink center.

Serves 6.

Source: *Florida Seafood: Yellowfin Tuna.* Tallahassee, FL: Florida Department of Natural Resources, no date.

Florida Orange Rice

Melt 3 tablespoons butter in heavy saucepan; add 1 cup diced celery and 2 tablespoons chopped onion; cook until onion is tender. Add 2 tablespoons slivered orange rind, 1½ cups water, 1 cup orange juice, 1½ teaspoons salt, ⅛ teaspoon thyme; bring to a boil. Add 1 cup rice; cover tightly and cook 25 minutes. Serve with roast duck, chicken, or ham.

6 servings.

Source: Florida Citrus Fare. Lakeland, FL: Florida Citrus Commission, no date.

Glazed Turkey Steaks

½ cup honey
⅓ cup grapefruit juice
3 tablespoons Dijon-style mustard
4 turkey steaks, cut from the breast, about ¾-inch thick
    (approximately 1 pound total)
2 grapefruit, peeled and sectioned

In a small bowl blend honey, grapefruit juice, and mustard. Arrange steaks on foil-lined, shallow broiler pan. Brush steaks lightly with honey mixture. Broil 6 inches from heat source, 6 minutes.

Turn, brush lightly, broil 6 minutes longer, just until juices run clear when meat is pierced with a fork. Meanwhile, heat remaining honey mixture over low heat in medium saucepan. Stir in grapefruit sections just before serving; heat 1 minute. Spoon sauce over steaks.

4 servings.

Source: *Taste the Tropics with Florida Grapefruit.* Lakeland, FL: Florida Department of Citrus, no date.

Grapefruit with Fish

Soak the fish in grapefruit juice ten or fifteen minutes before cooking. The tart juice will add a tang that counteracts the blandness of fish and that will give a distinguished flavor.

Source: *Florida Fruits and Vegetables in the Family Menu.* Bulletin No. 46, New Series, Tallahassee, FL: Florida Department of Agriculture, 1956.

Grilled Chicken and Florida Grapefruit Salad

½ cup frozen grapefruit juice concentrate, thawed

1 ripe banana, mashed

1 tablespoon olive oil

2 teaspoons red wine vinegar

¼ cup finely minced scallions

2 tablespoons chopped dill

2 cloves garlic, minced

1 teaspoon brown sugar

½ teaspoon salt

¼ teaspoon pepper

4 skinless, boneless chicken breast halves

4 cups mixed salad greens: Boston, romaine, red leaf

1 pint cherry tomatoes, halved

1 green pepper, cut into slivers

2 grapefruit, peeled and cut into ½-inch thick rounds

Preheat grill or broiler. In a medium bowl, combine grapefruit juice concentrate, banana, oil, vinegar, scallions, dill, garlic, sugar, salt, and pepper. Stir to combine. Place chicken in a shallow, non-metallic bowl. Divide marinade mixture, and pour half over the chicken. Marinate in refrigerator for 30 minutes, turning breasts over once. Place chicken on grill or broiler, 4 inches from the heat. Cook 5–7 minutes on each side, or until the chicken is cooked through. Remove to a plate, and set aside for 5 minutes. Divide and arrange salad greens, tomatoes, pepper, and grapefruit rounds on luncheon plates. Slice chicken diagonally, and place 1 chicken half on each plate. Drizzle any juices that have accumulated on the plate, and

Picking oranges at Largo, FL, near St. Petersburg, 1932. Floyd and Marion Rinhart Collection. Archives and Special Collections, University of Miami Library.

remaining dressing, over the chicken and salad greens. Garnish with additional dill and scallions, if desired.

4 servings.

Source: *Florida Citrus Cooking: Recipes from the Sunshine State.* Tallahassee, FL: Florida Department of Citrus, 1994.

Ham and Grapefruit

Peel and remove the sections and seeds from a large grapefruit. Cut the sections in halves lengthwise, then place them over the top of the almost-cooked ham. Sprinkle a thin layer of brown sugar over the fruit and finish cooking the ham.

Source: *Florida Fruits and Vegetables in the Family Menu.* Bulletin No. 46, New Series, Tallahassee, FL: Florida Department of Agriculture, 1956.

Lime Cocktail Sauce for Shellfish

1 tablespoon prepared horseradish
3 tablespoons tomato ketchup
1 teaspoon salt
6 tablespoons lime juice
¼ teaspoon Tabasco sauce
Oysters or clams

Mix sauce ingredients thoroughly and pour over oysters or clams arranged in cocktail glasses. Sauce may be served in baskets made from lemon rinds, the shellfish being served on the half shell. Serve very cold.

Source: Florida's Favorite Foods. Fruits and Vegetables in the Family Menu. Bulletin No. 46, Tallahassee, FL: Florida Department of Agriculture, 1959.

Lime with Fish

Squeeze juice of two limes over fish when ready to bake. Add more lime juice while fish are baking, if desired. Garnish with parsley and slice of lime.

Source: *Florida Fruits and Vegetables in the Family Menu.* Bulletin No. 46, New Series, Tallahassee, FL: Florida Department of Agriculture, 1956.

Mediterranean Pork Roast

1½ cups grapefruit juice
1 small red onion, finely chopped
1 clove garlic, minced
1 teaspoon sugar
1 teaspoon dried thyme or 1 tablespoon fresh thyme
1 teaspoon dried oregano or 1 tablespoon fresh oregano
2 pounds boneless pork tenderloin

In a non-metal casserole dish, combine grapefruit juice, red onion, garlic, sugar, thyme, and oregano. Add the pork tenderloin, cover and marinate 1 hour, turning pork once to ensure that it marinates evenly. Preheat oven to 425 degrees. Transfer the pork tenderloin with the onions and herb mixture to a roasting pan, reserving liquid from marinade. Place in oven, and roast 20 minutes. Reduce heat to 325 degrees, and continue roasting for one and half hours or until cooked through, basting occasionally with ½ cup of marinade. Remove pork from pan, and add remaining marinade to roasting pan, stirring until pan drippings loosen. Transfer mixture to small saucepan, and bring to boil, uncovered. Reduce heat and simmer 5–10 minutes. Slice pork, and serve with marinade.

6 servings.

Source: *Florida Citrus Cooking: Recipes from the Sunshine State.* Tallahassee, FL: Florida Department of Citrus, 1994.

Orange Beef Stir-Fry

2 oranges

1¼ pounds top round steak, trimmed

½ cup Florida orange juice, divided

2 tablespoons low-sodium soy sauce

1 tablespoon plus 1 teaspoon cornstarch

2 teaspoons brown sugar, divided

½ cup low-sodium chicken broth

1 tablespoon Oriental sesame oil

1 teaspoon finely minced ginger

1 clove garlic, minced

4 cups broccoli florets

4 medium scallions, cut into 2-inch pieces

1 8-ounce can sliced water chestnuts, rinsed and drained

3 tablespoons chopped cilantro

Using a paring knife or zester, remove rind from the oranges in thin strips. Set rind aside. Section peeled orange. Cut the round steak along grain into 2-inch wide strips. Thinly slice meat across grain into ¼-inch thick slices. Combine meat, 2 tablespoons orange juice, soy sauce, 1 tablespoon cornstarch, 1 teaspoon brown sugar and stir to combine. Set aside. In a small bowl, combine chicken broth and remaining orange juice, cornstarch and sugar. In a large non-stick skillet over medium-high heat, warm oil until hot, but not smoking. Add sliced meat, and stir-fry 3–4 minutes or until beef is browned but still slightly rare. Remove from skillet. Add ginger, garlic, orange rind, broccoli, scallions, water chestnuts and the chicken broth/orange juice mixture. Stir-fry 2–3 minutes, or until the vegetables begin to soften. Add cilantro and beef, including any juices that have accumulated, and cook, stirring until sauce has thickened slightly. Stir in orange sections, and serve immediately.

6 servings.

Source: *Florida Citrus Cooking: Recipes from the Sunshine State.* Tallahassee, FL: Florida Department of Citrus, 1994.

Orange Glazed Pork Chops

Quantity Serving

40 1-inch center cut pork chops
Salt and pepper
Paprika
10 ounces water
1 cup sugar
5 tablespoon cornstarch
1 tablespoon salt
1 tablespoon cinnamon
80 whole cloves
10 tablespoons grated orange rind
40 orange slices
5 cups orange juice

Family Serving

6 1-inch center cut pork chops
Salt and pepper
Paprika
½ cup water
1 tablespoon cornstarch
1 tablespoon salt
⅛ teaspoon cinnamon
12 whole cloves
3 tablespoons grated orange rind
20 orange slices
1 cup orange juice

Trim fat from chops and put in skillet over low heat. Let fry slowly until a thin coating of fat is in skillet. Sprinkle both sides generously with salt, pepper and paprika. Remove fat, brown chops well on both sides on medium heat. Spoon off fat, put on low heat, add water, and cover. Cook 45 minutes. Cook together sugar, cornstarch, salt, cinnamon, cloves, grated orange rind and orange juice until thickened. Spoon glaze over chops, cook 20 minutes. Garnish with orange slices and serve.

Source: *Famous Florida Chefs' Favorite Citrus Recipes.* Lakeland, FL: Florida Citrus Commission, no date.

Oriental Catfish Steaks

2 pounds Florida catfish steaks, fresh or frozen
¼ cup Florida orange juice
¼ cup soy sauce
2 tablespoons cooking oil or margarine, melted
2 tablespoons chopped Florida parsley
1 tablespoon Florida lemon juice
½ teaspoon oregano
½ teaspoon pepper
1 clove garlic minced

Thaw fish if frozen. Place fish in a single layer in a shallow dish. Combine remaining ingredients. Pour marinade over fish and let stand for 30 minutes in refrigerator, turning once. Remove fish, reserving marinade for basting. Place fish in a well-greased, hinged wire grill or on a well-greased broiler pan, approximately 13 × 10 inches. Cook over hot coals or under broiler, about 4 inches from source of heat, for 4 to 5 minutes. Turn and baste with marinade. Cook for 4 to 5 minutes more or until fish flakes easily when tested with a fork.

6 servings.

Source: *Florida Aquaculture Coast to Coast.* Tallahassee, FL: Florida Department of Agriculture and Consumer Services, no date.

Pineapple Omelet

7 eggs
1 teaspoon salt
3 tablespoons milk or cream
¾ cup grated cheese
1½ tablespoons butter
1½ cups crushed canned pineapple

Separate eggs; beat yolks for one minute; then add salt, milk or cream, and cheese and continue beating until well mixed. Melt butter in frying or omelet pan, turning pan so melted butter goes well up on the sides. Beat whites of eggs until stiff and fold in the yolk and cheese mixture. Pour into the pan and cook over low heat until nicely browned on the underside. Then place in a slow oven for about three minutes to dry off top. Meanwhile put the undrained pineapple into a sauce pan and boil until thick, about ten minutes. When omelet is done, make a cut about one and one-half inches long on either end of the fold line; then pour pineapple on one-half of the omelet, fold and slide onto platter.

Source: *Florida Fruits and Vegetables in the Family Menu.* Bulletin No. 46, New Series, Tallahassee, FL: Florida Department of Agriculture, 1956.

Polynesian Florida Yellowfin Tuna Steaks

2 pounds Florida yellowfin tuna steaks, fresh or frozen
⅓ cup soy sauce
1 can (8 ounces) unsweetened, crushed pineapple
2 tablespoons ketchup
2 tablespoons vegetable oil
2 tablespoons finely chopped parsley
1 tablespoon lemon juice
1 clove garlic, finely chopped
½ teaspoon oregano
½ teaspoon pepper

Thaw steaks, if frozen. Cut steaks into serving size portions. Place fish in single layer in a shallow dish. Combine all remaining ingredients. Pour sauce over fish and marinate in refrigerator for one hour turning once. Remove fish, reserving marinade for basting; place fish on a well-greased broiler pan. Broil about 4 inches from source of heat for 3 to 4 minutes. Turn carefully and baste with remaining marinade. Broil an additional 3 minutes longer, or until tuna has a slightly pink center.

6 servings.

Source: *Florida Seafood: Yellowfin Tuna.* Tallahassee, FL: Florida Department of Natural Resources, no date.

Snapper Fillets with Orange-Shallot Sauce

2 oranges
6 red snapper fillets, about 2¼ pounds
1 tablespoon olive oil
1 cup finely chopped shallots
2 cloves garlic, minced
3 tablespoons flour
1 cup chicken broth
1 cup Florida orange juice
1 tablespoon grated orange zest
2 tablespoons sherry
1½ teaspoons dried oregano
Salt and pepper, to taste
2 tablespoons chopped parsley, for garnish

Preheat broiler. Thinly slice the oranges into rounds and set aside. Place snapper fillets, skin side down, on a nonstick pan. Place 4 inches from the broiler, and broil 5–8 minutes or until fish flakes when tested with a fork. Remove from broiler, and set aside. Meanwhile, in a large, non-stick skillet, heat oil over medium-high heat until hot, but not smoking. Add shallots and garlic, and cook, stirring 3–4 minutes, or until shallots begin to brown. Add flour and cook, stirring until flour is no longer visible, about 30 seconds. Stir in chicken broth, orange juice, orange zest, sherry, oregano, salt, and pepper. Bring to a boil, stirring constantly, until slightly thickened. Add orange slices and fish fillets, skin side up. Cook 1–2 minutes, until fish is heated through and orange slices are slightly softened. Garnish with chopped parsley. Serve immediately.

Makes 6 servings.

Source: *Florida Citrus Cooking: Recipes from the Sunshine State.* Tallahassee, FL: Florida Department of Citrus, 1994.

Southern Fried Chicken a L'Orange

Marinate chicken in Valencia orange or Temple orange juice for one day. Follow your favorite Southern Fried Chicken recipe. Take one cup of leftover juice, and 1 cup of chicken stock, thicken with butter and flour. Serve on the side. Garnish your plate with heated (just warm) orange sections, corn fritters, or strips of bacon.

Source: *Famous Florida Chefs' Favorite Citrus Recipes*. Lakeland, FL: Florida Citrus Commission, no date.

Tangerine Sweet Potatoes

Add tangerine sections to candied sweet potatoes the last 10 minutes of baking just enough to heat through.

Source: *Florida Citrus Fare*. Lakeland, FL: Florida Citrus Commission, no date.

Cakes

Blueberry Cup Cakes

1 cup blueberries
1¼ cups flour
½ cup sugar
2 teaspoons baking powder
2 eggs
½ cup evaporated milk
½ teaspoon salt
¼ cup butter

Separate egg yolks and whites; cream butter and sugar, add milk and well-beaten egg yolks. Beat thoroughly. Sift baking powder, salt, and flour together; add berries. Combine all ingredients and fold into beaten egg whites. Pour in buttered muffin pans and bake for 25 or 30 minutes.

Source: *Florida Blueberries*. Bulletin No. 13-B, New Series, Tallahassee, FL: Florida Department of Agriculture, 1950.

Florida Coffee Cake

3 cups all-purpose flour
2 teaspoons baking powder
1 teaspoon baking soda
½ teaspoon salt
1 cup butter
2 cups sugar
2 eggs
1 banana, mashed
1 cup sweet potatoes, cooked and mashed
1 cup orange juice

Spray a bundt pan with baker's spray and dust with flour; set aside. Sift together flour, baking powder, soda and salt; set aside. Cream butter and sugar. Add eggs and beat until well blended; add banana and sweet potatoes and continue beating for 2 minutes. Alternately add dry ingredients and orange juice to the butter mixture, starting and ending with flour.

Topping and Filling

½ cup butter, melted
1 cup sugar
1 cup pecans, chopped
1 cup coconut, shredded and toasted
1 tablespoon orange peel, grated

Melt butter, add remaining ingredients, and mix well. Put ⅓ of topping in bundt pan, spread evenly. Top with half of batter. Smooth with spatula and make a slight channel in center of ring. Fill with remainder of topping. Carefully spoon batter over topping, making sure batter touches each side of cake pan (to seal in filling). Bake at 350 degrees for 45 minutes, or until toothpick comes out clean.

Source: *Florida Holiday Recipes*. Tallahassee, FL: Florida Department of Agriculture and Consumer Services, 1990.

*Tall coconut palms, Palm
Beach, 1923. Floyd and Marion
Rinhart Collection. Archives
and Special Collections,
University of Miami Library.*

Florida Orange Ambrosia Cake

2 cups sifted cake flour
1⅓ cups sugar
2 teaspoons baking powder
¼ teaspoon baking soda
1 teaspoon salt
⅔ cup shortening
½ cup orange juice
3 eggs

Sift flour, sugar, baking powder, soda, and salt into mixing bowl.
Add shortening and orange juice. Beat 2 minutes or 200 strokes. Add

eggs. Beat 2 minutes more. Turn into 2 greased 9-inch round cake pans. Bake in moderate oven, 375 degrees, 25 to 30 minutes. Spread with Orange Frosting; garnish with orange sections.

Orange Frosting

3 egg whites
4 cups sifted confectioners' sugar
2 teaspoons orange juice
2 teaspoons grated orange rind

Beat egg whites until stiff. Add sugar, orange juice, and grated rind. Blend well and spread on cake.

Source: *Florida's Favorite Recipes for Citrus Fruits. A compilation of recipes which won top honors in county contests jointly sponsored by the Florida Agricultural Extension Service, home demonstration work, and the Florida Chain Store Council as a feature of Florida's "Eat More Citrus Month," February, 1954.* Lakeland, FL: Florida Citrus Commission, 1954.

Florida Orange Chiffon Cake

½ cup shortening
1½ cups sugar
1 teaspoon lemon juice
2 tablespoons grated orange rind
2½ cups sifted flour
3 teaspoons baking powder
½ teaspoon salt
1 cup orange juice
½ cup (or 4) egg whites

Cream shortening, sugar, and lemon juice together until fluffy. Blend in grated orange rind. Sift flour, baking powder, and salt together. Add to creamed mixture in three portions alternately with orange juice in two portions, beating after each addition. Beat egg whites until stiff but not dry. Fold into batter. Turn into a tube cake pan. Bake in moderate oven, 350 degrees, 45 to 60 minutes. Allow cake to cool in pan. When cake is cool, remove from pan and place on baking sheet. Split cake crosswise into 3 layers. Spread filling between layers, reserving small amount for garnish. Spread meringue on top and bake 8–10 minutes in 400 degree oven.

Orange Filling

1½ cups sugar
4½ tablespoons cornstarch
½ teaspoon salt
1½ cups fresh orange juice
2 tablespoons lemon juice
4 egg yolks, slightly beaten
3 tablespoons grated orange rind
3 tablespoons butter

Mix sugar, cornstarch, salt, orange juice and lemon juice together in a saucepan. Cook over low heat, stirring constantly, until the cornstarch is cooked and clear. Add egg yolks and cook about 1 minute longer. Remove from heat. Blend in grated orange rind and butter. Chill, then spread between cake layers.

Meringue

4 egg whites
¾ cup sugar
¼ teaspoon cream of tartar

Beat egg whites and cream of tartar until eggs are frothy. Gradually beat in sugar until mixture is stiff but not dry.

Source: *Florida's Favorite Recipes for Citrus Fruits. A compilation of recipes which won top honors in county contests jointly sponsored by the Florida Agricultural Extension Service, home demonstration work, and the Florida Chain Store Council as a feature of Florida's "Eat More Citrus Month," February, 1954.* Lakeland, FL: Florida Citrus Commission, 1954.

Florida Orange Suncakes with Blueberry Orange Sauce

2 large eggs, separated
⅔ cup nonfat ricotta cheese
¼ cup low-fat milk
6 tablespoons all-purpose flour
1 tablespoon grated orange zest
2 teaspoons sugar
¼ teaspoon baking powder
Pinch of salt
1 tablespoon vegetable oil
Blueberry Orange Sauce

Add egg yolks and ricotta cheese to food processor or blender and process until smooth. Add milk, flour, orange zest, sugar, baking powder, and salt; process until completely blended. In a large bowl, beat egg whites until stiff, but not dry; fold into batter. In a large non-stick skillet, heat oil over medium heat. Drop ¼ cup of batter onto skillet. Cook until tops are bubbly and look dry, about 3 minutes; turn and cook second side until golden brown, 1-2 minutes. Repeat with remaining batter. Serve hot with Blueberry Orange Sauce.

Blueberry Orange Sauce

1 cup fresh or thawed frozen blueberries
2 tablespoon Florida orange juice
1 tablespoon sugar
1 teaspoon grated orange zest

In a medium saucepan, heat all the ingredients over medium fire, stirring frequently until thick and syrupy, 5-7 minutes. Pour over Florida Orange Suncakes.

Makes 12 suncakes.

Source: *Florida Citrus Cooking: Recipes from the Sunshine State.* Tallahassee, FL: Florida Department of Citrus, 1994.

Florida Snowflakes

½ cup butter
½ cup shortening
1 cup sugar
2 large eggs
1 tablespoon lime rind, grated
2 teaspoons Florida lime juice
1 teaspoon vanilla extract
½ teaspoon almond extract
3½ cups all-purpose flour
½ teaspoon baking powder
½ teaspoon salt
⅓ cup strawberry jam
1 cup powdered sugar, sifted

Beat butter and shortening at medium speed with an electric mixer until soft and creamy; gradually add sugar, beating well. Add eggs, lime rind. Add lime juice and extracts, mixing well. Sift together flour, baking powder, and salt; gradually add to butter mixture, mixing well. Cover; chill 1 hour.

Divide dough in half; store one portion in refrigerator. Roll remaining dough to ⅛-inch thickness on a lightly floured surface. Cut with a 2½ inch star-shaped cookie cutter, and place on ungreased cookie sheets. Bake at 375 degrees for 7 to 8 minutes or until lightly browned; cool 2 minutes on cookie sheet. Remove to wire racks to cool. Repeat with remaining dough.

Just before serving, spread center of half of cookies with about ¼ teaspoon strawberry jam. Place a second cookie on top, alternating points of stars of top and bottom cookies. Sprinkle generously with powdered sugar.

5 dozen.

Source: *Holiday Recipes Fresh from Florida.* Tallahassee, FL: Florida Department of Agriculture and Consumer Services, no date.

Fresh Strawberry Cake

1 1-pound, 2½ ounce box yellow cake mix
1 3-ounce package strawberry jello
½ cup salad oil
¼ cup water or berry juice
3 eggs
1 cup strawberries, crushed
½ cup butter
1 1-pound box confectioners' sugar, sifted
½ cup strawberries, crushed

Empty cake mix into large bowl of mixer. Add next four ingredients and mix thoroughly with electric beater. Stir in crushed fresh strawberries. Pour into two 9-inch paper-lined cake pans. Bake in 350 degree oven 30 to 35 minutes or until done. Let cake cool before icing. For the icing, thoroughly cream butter and sugar together. Stir in berries; mix well. Spread icing onto cake.

Source: *Florida Recipes*. Tallahassee, FL: Florida Department of Agriculture and Consumer Services, no date.

Grapefruit Quick Shortcake

Sections of 1 grapefruit
Canned peaches
4 tablespoons powdered sugar
Maraschino cherries
4 tablespoons shredded coconut
¼ cup heavy cream
Loaf sponge cake

Use individual plates and arrange 1 slice of cake on each plate. Allow 2 sections grapefruit and 2 sections peach to each serving.

Arrange fruits alternately in each of the four corners of cake slice. Sprinkle fruits with sugar and shredded coconut. Pile sweetened whipped cream in center space and top with Maraschino garnish. (Canned apricots and pears and thin sections of canned pineapple can be similarly used with grapefruit sections).

Source: *Florida Fruits and Vegetables in the Family Menu.* Bulletin No. 46, New Series, Tallahassee, FL: Florida Department of Agriculture, 1956.

Mango Upside-Down Cake

2 cups sliced ripe mangos
2 tablespoons lemon juice
1 tablespoon margarine
⅓ cup brown sugar
¼ cup shortening
¾ cup sugar
1 egg
½ cup milk
1¼ cups flour
2 teaspoons baking powder
¼ teaspoon salt

Pour lemon juice over mangos and let stand 15 minutes. Melt margarine in 8-inch round pan. (Do not use iron skillet as mangos will darken.) Add brown sugar and cover with mango slices. To prepare cake batter, creamshortening; add beaten egg. Sift dry ingredients and add alternately with milk. Pour over mangos and bake 50 to 60 minutes at 375 degrees. When cake is done, turn upside down and serve while warm.

Source: *Florida Fruit and Vegetable Recipes.* Tallahassee, FL: Florida Department of Agriculture, no date.

Orange Honey Coconut Cake

½ cup shortening
½ cup sugar
½ cup orange honey
5 egg yolks
1¾ cups all-purpose flour
3 teaspoons baking powder
½ teaspoons salt
⅝ cup milk
1 tablespoon grated orange rind
1 tablespoon orange juice

Cream shortening; add sugar gradually and cream well. Add honey and mix well; add the very well-beaten egg yolks. Sift flour once before measuring. Sift flour, baking powder, and salt together. Add to creamed mixture alternately with the milk. Add orange rind and juice. Bake in well-greased and floured pan for 40 minutes in moderate oven (350 degrees). Ice with Honey Coconut Meringue.

Honey Coconut Meringue Icing

⅓ cup honey
Dash salt
2 egg whites
½ cup toasted coconut

Heat honey to 240 degrees, or until it spins an 8-inch thread. Pour slowly into stiffly beaten egg whites and beat with egg beater constantly. Add salt and continue beating until mixture is fluffy and will hold its shape. Spread on warm cake and sprinkle top with the coconut, lightly toasted. Place pan of cake on board or in another pan to prevent further browning and return cake to oven to set meringue. Bake 10 minutes at 250 degrees. To toast coconut: place 1 package coconut and 2 teaspoons butter in pan and toast very slowly in oven, stirring frequently to prevent burning.

Source: *Florida Honey and Its Hundred Uses.* Bulletin No. 66, Tallahassee, FL: Florida Department of Agriculture, 1933.

Orange Ice Box Cake

1 cup sugar
2 tablespoons cornstarch
⅛ teaspoon salt
2 cups milk
2 eggs (or 4 egg yolks)
1 tablespoon gelatin
2 tablespoons cold water
¾ cup fresh orange juice
1 tablespoon grated orange rind
1 pint whipping cream
2 packages ladyfingers
1 package walnut halves

Mix sugar, cornstarch and salt. Add milk gradually, then beaten eggs. Cook in double boiler until thick. Soak gelatin in cold water, then dissolve in hot custard. When cold, add fruit juice, rind, and whipped cream. Line a springform pan with ladyfingers. Fill with pudding. Chill. When firm remove rings of pan, decorate with additional whipped cream, orange sections and walnuts.

Source: *Famous Florida Chefs' Favorite Citrus Recipes.* Lakeland, FL: Florida Citrus Commission, no date.

Orange Layer Cake

½ cup butter
1 cup sugar
3 whole eggs
1 teaspoon grated orange rind
2 cups sifted cake flour
3 teaspoons baking powder
½ teaspoon salt
⅓ cup orange juice

Cream butter and sugar. Beat in eggs one at a time. Blend in grated orange rind. Sift together flour, baking powder, and salt. Add to creamed mixture in 3 portions alternately with orange juice in two portions. Turn batter into two greased 9-inch layer pans. Bake in moderate oven, 375 degrees, 20 to 25 minutes or until done. Remove from oven. Let set in pan 10 minutes. Turn out onto cooling rack or cake plate.

Orange Filling

4 tablespoons flour
1½ cups sugar
¼ teaspoon salt
1 cup orange juice
1 cup orange pulp
3 egg yolks, beaten
2 tablespoons butter
1 teaspoon lemon juice
½ cup grated coconut

Combine flour, sugar, salt, orange juice and pulp. Cook over hot water until flour is cooked. Stir in beaten egg yolks and cook until thick. Add butter, lemon juice and coconut. Cool and spread between layers of cake.

Ambrosia Icing

3 egg whites
6 tablespoons water
1½ cups sugar
¼ teaspoon salt
¼ teaspoon cream of tartar
1 teaspoon vanilla
Coconut and orange sections for garnishing

Combine and cook over hot water, beating constantly, until mixture stands in peaks. Remove from heat. Add vanilla. Beat until cool. Spread on tops and sides of cakes. Sprinkle coconut over top and garnish with orange sections.

15 to 20 servings.

Source: *Florida's Favorite Recipes for Citrus Fruits. A compilation of recipes which won top honors in county contests jointly sponsored by the Florida Agricultural Extension Service, home demonstration work, and the Florida Chain Store Council as a feature of Florida's "Eat More Citrus Month,"* February, 1954. Lakeland, FL: Florida Citrus Commission, 1954.

Papaya Sauce Cake

1 cup diced ripe papaya
3 tablespoons water
¼ cup shortening
1 cup sugar
1 egg
1¼ teaspoons baking powder
½ teaspoon salt
⅓ teaspooon each ground cinnamon and nutmeg
¼ teaspoon ground ginger
1¼ cups flour
2 teaspoon lemon juice
½ cup seedless raisins (optional)

Stew the papaya and water together until a smooth sauce is obtained; press the mixture through a coarse sieve if necessary. Cream shortening. Add sugar and mix well. Add beaten egg. Sift dry ingredients. Add cooled papaya sauce and the dry ingredients alternately to egg mixture. Fold in lemon juice and raisins. Pour into oiled loaf-pan and bake in a moderate oven, 350 degrees, for 50-60 minutes.

Source: *Florida Fruit and Vegetable Recipes.* Tallahassee, FL: Florida Department of Agriculture, no date.

Sunshine Cake with Ambrosia Frosting

¾ cup butter or margarine
1 cup sugar
1 tablespoon grated orange rind
1 teaspoon vanilla, 3 eggs
1 cup orange marmalade
½ cup raisins
3 cups sifted all-purpose flour
1½ teaspoons soda 1 teaspoon salt
1 cup buttermilk

Cream together butter, sugar, orange rind, and vanilla until fluffy. Add eggs, one at a time, beating well after each addition. Stir in marmalade and raisins. Sift together flour, baking soda, and salt. Add to first mixture alternately with buttermilk. Turn batter into a greased and lined 9-inch tube pan. Bake in a moderate oven, 350 degrees, 1 hour. Cool cake in pan for 10 minutes; remove from pan.

Ambrosia Frosting

Mix 1½ cups sugar, 2 egg whites, 5 tablespoons orange juice, and ⅛ teaspoon salt in top of double boiler. Beat with rotary beater until sugar is dissolved. Place over boiling water and cook, beating constantly for 7 minutes, or until frosting stands in peaks. Remove from heat; add 2 teaspoons grated orange rind and beat until thick enough to spread. Garnish with shredded coconut and orange sections. Yields enough to fill and frost 2 8-inch or 9-inch layers.

12 servings.

Source: *Florida Fruit and Vegetable Recipes.* Tallahassee, FL: Florida Department of Agriculture, no date.

Tasty Fruit Bars

Filling

2 tablespoons flour
¾ cup sugar
1 cup raisins, ground
1 cup cooked prunes, drained and chopped
1½ cups orange juice

Mix flour with sugar. Blend all ingredients together. Cook until thick. Set aside to cool.

Crust

¾ cup butter and shortening
1 cup brown sugar
1¾ cups sifted flour
½ teaspoon baking soda
1 teaspoon salt
1½ cups quick cooking oatmeal

Mix butter, shortening, and sugar thoroughly. Sift flour, soda, and salt together. Add oatmeal. Blend to make crumb mixture. Press ½ of crumb mixture evenly into greased and floured 9 × 13 × 2 inch pan. Spread with cooled filling. Spread with remaining crumb mixture, patting lightly. Bake in a hot oven, 400 degrees, 25 to 30 minutes or until lightly browned. Cut into bars while warm.

2 dozen bars.

Source: *Florida's Favorite Recipes for Citrus Fruits. A compilation of recipes which won top honors in county contests jointly sponsored by the Florida Agricultural Extension Service, home demonstration work, and the Florida Chain Store Council as a feature of Florida's "Eat More Citrus Month," February, 1954.* Lakeland, FL: Florida Citrus Commission, 1954.

Upside-Down Cake

½ pound butter
1½ cups sugar
3 eggs
2 tablespoons baking powder
2½ cups pastry flour
1 cup grapefruit juice
3 cups grapefruit pulp

Grease pan thickly with butter. Place three cups grapefruit pulp in pan, with one cup brown sugar. Mix batter in the usual way and pour over the grapefruit in pan. Bake for about fifty minutes. May be served with whipped cream if desired.

Source: *Florida Fruits and Vegetables in the Family Menu.* Bulletin No. 46, New Series, Tallahassee, FL: Florida Department of Agriculture, 1956.

Cookies

Drop Cookies

1 cup shortening
¼ cup sugar
½ cup strained honey
2 cups flour
2 eggs
½ teaspoon baking soda
½ teaspoon salt
½ teaspoon vanilla
2 drops almond extract
½ cup nut meats
½ cup raisins

Cream shortening and sugar thoroughly. Add honey, beaten eggs, and flavoring. Sift flour, soda, and salt together and add to first mixture. Combine with lightly floured nuts and raisins. Drop by spoonfuls on oiled baking sheet. Bake in moderate oven, 350 to 375 degrees.

Source: *Florida Honey and Its Hundred Uses.* Bulletin No. 66, Tallahassee, FL: Florida Department of Agriculture, 1933.

Honey Cookies

½ cup butter
¾ cup sugar
1 egg and 1 egg yolk
½ cup honey
Grated rind of 1 lemon
3 cups flour
4 teaspoons baking powder
1 egg white (saved from above)
Pecans, chopped

Cream the butter and sugar together, and add the egg and egg yolk beaten together, the honey, lemon rind, and the flour sifted with the baking powder. More flour may be required. The dough should be stiff enough to be easily handled. Take a small portion of dough at a time, knead slightly, roll into a thin sheet and cut into cookies of any desired shape. Set the shapes on a greased pan. Beat the white of the egg a little; brush over the top of the cookies, then at once sprinkle on some finely chopped pecans and a little granulated sugar. Bake in a moderate oven (about 10 minutes at 350 degrees).

Source: *Florida Honey and Its Hundred Uses.* Bulletin No. 66, Tallahassee, FL: Florida Department of Agriculture, 1933.

Honey Fudge Squares

½ cup cocoa or 2 squares bitter chocolate

⅓ cup shortening

½ cup pecans or black walnuts

¼ teaspoon soda

Pinch salt

1 teaspoon baking powder

½ cup honey

½ cup brown sugar

1 cup chopped dates, or candied orange peel

1 egg

2 cups flour

¼ cup sour cream, or ¼ cup of evaporated milk to which has been added ¼ teaspoon vinegar

Melt chocolate over hot water if squares of chocolate are used. Blend the melted chocolate or cocoa with honey, brown sugar and shortening. Add 1 egg, then sour cream. Add sifted dry ingredients. Then add the nuts and dates or peel. Spread batter to about ½-inch depth in flat pan and bake in moderate oven about 35 minutes. When cool, cut in squares.

Source: *Florida Honey and Its Hundred Uses.* Bulletin No. 66, Tallahassee, FL: Florida Department of Agriculture, 1933.

Honey Oatmeal Cookies

1 cup honey
2-3 cups shortening
½ teaspoon salt
2 eggs, beaten
2 cups rolled oats
2 cups of flour
½ teaspoon soda
2 teaspoons baking powder
1 teaspoon cinnamon
1 cup chopped raisins

Cream the shortening and honey together, then add the eggs. Mix and sift the flour, soda, baking powder, cinnamon, and salt, and add to the wet mixture together with oatmeal. Dust the raisins with some of the flour and add them to the dough, mixing well. Drop by teaspoonfuls on a greased pan. Bake in a moderate oven 10 to 12 minutes.

Source: *Florida Honey and Its Hundred Uses.* Bulletin No. 66, Tallahassee, FL: Florida Department of Agriculture, 1933.

Lemon Nut Drop Cookies

½ cup butter
2 egg yolks, beaten
Grated rind of one lemon
3 tablespoons lemon juice
3½ cups flour
2 egg whites, whipped
½ cup sugar
1 teaspoon salt
1 cup honey
Shredded coconut

Cream the butter, beat in the sugar and add the egg yolks and lemon. Then stir in three cups of flour and the salt and soda sifted together, alternately with the honey. Fold in the beaten egg whites and stir in the nut meats, floured with the remaining ¼ cup of flour. Drop by teaspoons onto a buttered baking pan two inches apart. Bake in a moderate oven, 350 degrees, from 15 to 25 minutes. Sprinkle with shredded coconut before baking.

Source: *Florida Honey and Its Hundred Uses.* Bulletin No. 66, Tallahassee, FL: Florida Department of Agriculture, 1933.

Lemon Thins

1 cup butter
½ cup sugar
½ cup brown sugar
2 tablespoons lemon juice
1 teaspoon grated lemon rind
3 to 3¼ cups sifted flour*
1 egg
1 teaspoon salt
¼ teaspoon soda

Cream butter and sugar. Add lemon juice, rind, and egg. Beat. Sift dry ingredients, add to egg mixture. Put through cookie press on ungreased cookie sheet. Or they may be dropped by teaspoonfuls and pressed flat with a glass or fork. Bake 400 degrees for 12 minutes.

*Three cups of flour should be enough, but if dough spreads too much in oven, add ¼ cup of flour to remainder of the dough.

6 to 7 dozen.

Source: *Using Florida Citrus Fruits.* Circular No. 231, Gainesville, FL: University of Florida Agricultural Extension Service, 1962.

Large orange packing plant at Lake Alfred, 1933. Floyd and Marion Rinhart Collection. Archives and Special Collections, University of Miami Library.

Orange Crisps

½ cup butter
1 cup sugar
1 egg
Grated rind of 1 lemon
Grated rind of 1 orange
3 cups sifted flour
3 tablespoons orange juice
¼ teaspoon soda
½ teaspoon baking powder

Cream butter, add sugar. Mix well. Beat in egg and orange juice. Sift dry ingredients together. Add to egg-sugar mixture. Add grated rind. Blend well. Shape in rolls and chill. Slice in ⅛-inch thick slices and bake at 375 degrees until crisp. May be forced through a cookie press if desired.

4 to 5 dozen.

Source: *Using Florida Citrus Fruits.* Circular No. 231, Gainesville, FL: University of Florida Agricultural Extension Service, 1962.

Orange Pecan Cookies

1½ cups shortening
¾ cup brown sugar
¾ cup granulated sugar
1 large egg, unbeaten
¾ cup chopped nuts
¼ cup grated orange rind
¼ cup orange juice
4 cups flour, plus 2 tablespoons
¼ teaspoon baking soda
¼ teaspoon salt

Combine shortening and sugar. Add egg, salt, grated rind, and juice. Beat well. Sift baking soda and flour together. Add to the mixture and blend well. Add nuts. Shape into rolls 2 inches across. Wrap in waxed paper and chill several hours. Slice ¼ inch thick. Bake at 400 degrees, 8 to 10 minutes.

5 dozen.

Source: *Using Florida Citrus Fruits.* Circular No. 231, Gainesville, FL: University of Florida Agricultural Extension Service, 1962.

Orange Snow Cloud Cookies

¼ cup softened shortening

4 tablespoons of light brown sugar

3 tablespoons of granulated sugar

1 large egg, beaten lightly

1 teaspoon vanilla

2 tablespoons grated orange rind

1 cup finely diced Florida Temple orange (or Florida orange of your choice)

2 cups all-purpose flour

1 teaspoon baking powder

½ teaspoon baking soda

¼ teaspoon salt

⅓ cup flaked coconut

Sifted confectioners sugar for garnish

Preheat oven to 350 degrees. In a bowl, cream the shortening with the sugars until light and fluffy. Add the egg, a little at a time, and beat until well combined. Beat in the vanilla and the orange rind. Stir in the diced orange.

In a bowl, sift the flour, baking powder, baking soda and salt. Add the flour mixture to the orange mixture and stir until combined well. Fold in the coconut.

With a tablespoon, drop the batter onto lightly greased baking sheets (spacing them 1½ inches apart) and bake the cookies in the oven for 12 minutes, or until pale golden. Cool on racks to room temperature, and sprinkle with the confectioners' sugar.

Source: *Florida Citrus Cooking: Recipes from the Sunshine State.* Tallahassee, FL: Florida Department of Citrus, 1994.

Desserts

Ambrosia No. 1

6 oranges
½ cup sugar
3 cups fresh grated coconut

Peel and slice pulp of oranges. Grate coconut. Place a layer of orange pulp in a large bowl. Sprinkle a little sugar and add a layer of coconut, then another layer of orange, a sprinkle of sugar, and over all pour coconut juice and fresh orange juice. Add a final covering of grated coconut. Leave in refrigerator until next day and serve.

Source: *Florida Fruits and Vegetables in the Family Menu.* Bulletin No. 46, New Series, Tallahassee, FL: Florida Department of Agriculture, 1956.

Ambrosia No. 2

1 grapefruit, sectioned
2 oranges, sectioned
½ cup shredded coconut
2 tablespoons sugar
4 sprigs mint

Alternate layers of mixed grapefruit and orange sections with coconut. Sprinkle each layer lightly with sugar. Chill in refrigerator one hour before serving. Garnish with mint. Optional: use 2 additional oranges and omit grapefruit.

4 servings.

Source: *Using Florida Citrus Fruits.* Circular No. 231, Gainesville, FL: University of Florida Agricultural Extension Service, 1962.

Baked Grapefruit

Cut grapefruit in half, cut around sections, and cut small hole in center. Fill center cavity until overflowing with honey and one teaspoon of butter. Sprinkle over entire top of fruit, a mixture of sugar and cinnamon. Put under broiler for a few moments until it turns a little brown. Garnish with a grilled chicken liver.

1 serving.

Source: *Famous Florida Chefs' Favorite Citrus Recipes.* Lakeland, FL: Florida Citrus Commission, no date.

Baked Grapefruit Souffle

½ cup grapefruit pulp
½ cup orange pulp
2 egg whites
1 cup sugar
1 teaspoon flour
⅛ teaspoon salt

Rub fruit pulp through sieve; add sugar, salt and heat. Fold stiffly beaten egg whites into hot fruit pulp. Fill greased baking dish or small molds three-quarters full of mixture and set in a pan of hot water. Bake in slow oven about 25 minutes until firm. Serve with whipped cream or with grapefruit sauce.

Source: *Florida Fruits and Vegetables in the Family Menu.* Bulletin No. 46, New Series, Tallahassee, FL: Florida Department of Agriculture, 1956.

Baked Papaya

1 small firm ripe papaya
1 tablespoon butter
¾ teaspoon salt
2 tablespoons lemon juice

Pare and cut papaya lengthwise into six pieces, remove seeds. Sprinkle with salt, lemon juice, and butter. Place in a baking pan, add enough water to cover bottom of pan to prevent burning, and bake in a moderate oven (350 degrees) for 35 minutes. Serve immediately after removing from the oven. This may be used in place of a vegetable.

Source: *The Papaya. A Fruit Suitable for South Florida.* Bulletin No. 90, New Series, Tallahassee, FL: Florida Department of Agriculture, 1939.

Baked Pears

Core firm, medium-sized pears. Place in covered baking dish, sprinkle with brown sugar. Add stick of cinnamon. Allow enough water to cover bottom of pan. When tender, transfer pears to glass dish, cook down syrup from baking dish and pour over pears. Serve hot or cold.

Source: *Florida Fruits and Vegetables in the Family Menu.* Bulletin No. 46, New Series, Tallahassee, FL: Florida Department of Agriculture, 1956.

Broiled Grapefruit No. 1

Cut each grapefruit in half, core, and remove seeds. Sprinkle one tablespoon brown sugar over the top of each half. Place three cherries in the center and add a little of juice. Preheat the oven broiler for about ten minutes. Place the grapefruit under the flame for seven to ten minutes. The sugar will melt and spread to give the grapefruit a lovely browned surface, and a delightful flavor.

Source: *Florida Fruits and Vegetables in the Family Menu.* Bulletin No. 46, New Series, Tallahassee, FL: Florida Department of Agriculture, 1956.

Broiled Grapefruit No. 2

Sprinkle each half with 1 tablespoon sugar and a dash or cinnamon, mace, or nutmeg, if desired. Dot with 1 teaspoon butter. Place grapefruit on broiler rack 3 inches from heat. Broil slowly 15 to 20 minutes or until grapefruit is slightly brown and heated through. Grapefruit may also be baked in a moderately hot oven (400 degrees) 15 to 20 minutes. Serve hot.

Source: *Florida Citrus Fare.* Lakeland, FL: Florida Citrus Commission, no date.

Broiled Grapefruit No. 3

Halve grapefruit and loosen sections by running a stainless steel knife between each section and membrane on each side. Place halves on broiler pan and top with:

Brown sugar: It melts to sweeten all the fruit. A splash of sherry or orange juice starts the sugar melting.

Honey: Sweetens the fruit without caramelizing on top.

Cinnamon sugar: Sprinkle on generously.

Place grapefruit halves under broiler for 3 to 5 minutes. Garnish with thin slices of apple, strawberries in season, or cherries.

Source: *Florida Citrus Sampler.* Lakeland, FL: Florida Department of Citrus, no date.

Broiled Grapefruit No. 4

1 grapefruit
¼ cup finely chopped pecans
2 teaspoons sugar
¼ teaspoon cinnamon

Mix pecans, sugar, and cinnamon. Sprinkle on grapefruit halves. Let stand 5 minutes. Broil by placing grapefruit halves on broiler rack 3 inches from heat. Broil 15 to 20 minutes, or until grapefruit is heated through.

Source: *Florida's Favorite Recipes for Citrus Fruits. A compilation of recipes which won top honors in county contests jointly sponsored by the Florida Agricultural Extension Service, home demonstration work, and the Florida Chain Store Council as a feature of Florida's "Eat More Citrus Month," February, 1954.* Lakeland, FL: Florida Citrus Commission, 1954.

Cinnamon Oranges

4 oranges
1 teaspoon cinnamon
½ cup granulated, powdered or sifted confectioners' sugar

Cut off orange peel in a long strip going around orange and cutting deep enough to remove white membrane. Combine cinnamon and sugar. Spear oranges on fork; roll in sugar mixture.

4 servings.

Source: *Florida Fruit and Vegetable Recipes.* Tallahassee, FL: Florida Department of Agriculture, no date.

Citus Dessert Tray

2 grapefruit (one pink, if possible)
2 oranges
6 tangerines
¼ pound sharp cheddar cheese
¼ pound Swiss cheese
¼ pound crisp crackers
Mint

Wash fruit, section grapefruit. Peel and cut oranges into 6 slices each. With a sharp paring knife, cut peel of tangerine from top down to ¼ inch from stem and into six sections. Be careful not to cut too far down. Pull "petals" of peel up and fold in under fruit. Gently separate sections and place whole fruit on tray or large plate. Arrange grapefruit sections and orange slices on same tray. Cube cheeses and place on tray. Garnish with mint. Serve with crisp crackers.

Serves 6 to 8.

Source: *Using Florida Citrus Fruits.* Circular No. 231, Gainesville, FL: University of Florida Agricultural Extension Service, 1962.

Dream Boats

½ cup grapefruit pulp
½ cup orange pulp
½ cup white grapes
Remainder of banana pulp that has been scooped out to make boats
Few shredded nut meats

Moisten fruit mixture with French dressing and place in banana boats, garnishing with sliced maraschino cherries, and serve with hot crackers.

One banana for each person served. Cut lengthwise and arrange both sections on crisp lettuce.

Source: *Florida Fruits and Vegetables in the Family Menu*. Bulletin No. 46, New Series, Tallahassee, FL: Florida Department of Agriculture, 1956.

Florida Floating Island

Use 2½ cups of citrus juice in preparing packaged vanilla pudding. Pour pudding into serving dishes. Cool. Beat 1 egg white until stiff, gradually beat in 2 tablespoons sugar; add ½ teaspoon vanilla. Top each serving with a spoonful of the meringue. (If a cooked meringue is desired, drop meringue by spoonfuls into a shallow baking pan with the bottom just covered with hot water.) Bake in moderate oven (350 degrees) about 10 minutes.

6 servings.

Source: *Florida Citrus Fare*. Lakeland, FL: Florida Citrus Commission, no date.

Florida Grapefruit Mousse

¼ cup plus 1 tablespoon frozen grapefruit juice concentrate, thawed
    and divided
1 teaspoon plain gelatin
1 tablespoon sugar
2 grapefruit
¾ cup evaporated whole or skim milk, chilled
3 tablespoons powdered sugar

In a small saucepan, combine 2 tablespoons grapefruit juice concentrate and gelatin, stirring until gelatin softens. Add sugar and 2 more tablespoons of concentrate, and place saucepan over medium heat, stirring constantly until just dissolved, about 3–5 minutes. Remove from heat, and allow to cool. Meanwhile, peel grapefruit and remove white pith. Section grapefruit, removing membrane that separates the fruit segments. Cut fruit into bite-size pieces. Beat evaporated milk until frothy. Add remaining tablespoon of grapefruit juice concentrate, and continue beating until mixture becomes stiff. Add powdered sugar and beat 10 more seconds until combined. Fold mixture into gelatin until combined. Fold fruit into mousse mixture, and turn into parfait glasses. Serve immediately or chill. (Because the mousse is a beaten dessert, it should be prepared the same day it is to be served).

Makes 6 servings.

Source: *Florida Citrus Cooking: Recipes from the Sunshine State.* Tallahassee, FL: Florida Department of Citrus, 1994.

Florida Lollipops

Pour orange or tangerine juice into freezing tray of refrigerator with cube divisions left in. Freeze until almost firm. Insert ice cream sticks into the center of each cube. Return to freezer and freeze until firm.

16 lollipops.

Source: *Florida Citrus Fare.* Lakeland, FL: Florida Citrus Commission, no date.

Florida Watermelon Sundae

2 cups watermelon cubes about ½″ × ½″
1 20-ounce can crushed pineapple
Vanilla ice cream

Drain pineapple well; save juice for syrup. Place watermelon in sherbet glass or small bowl. Place a scoop of ice cream in each bowl. Spoon pineapple over this and top with syrup.

Syrup

Place ¾ cup pineapple juice from crushed pineapple in saucepan. Add 1 tablespoon of confectioners sugar and 2 teaspoons of cornstarch. Boil and stir for 15 minutes. Let cool and pour over ice cream.

Source: *Florida Recipes*. Tallahassee, FL: Florida Department of Agriculture and Consumer Services, no date.

Fresh Sliced Mangos

One of the most popular mango desserts is the freshly sliced fruit served either plain or with a few drops of lime juice squeezed over the cut fruit.

Source: *Mangos in Florida*. Tallahassee, FL: Florida Department of Agriculture, in cooperation with University of Miami, Coral Gables, FL, 1950.

Frozen Lime Dessert

3 tablespoons butter, melted

1 cup fine graham cracker crumbs (12 2½-inch squares)

2 eggs, separated

¼ cup sugar

1 15-ounce can sweetened condensed milk

⅔ cup lime juice, or 1 can (6 ounces) frozen concentrated limeade

1 tablespoon lime rind

Combine butter and graham cracker crumbs. Press ⅔ cup of crumb mixture on bottom and sides of a lightly buttered ice tray; chill. Beat egg yolks until thick; combine with condensed milk. Stir in lime rind and juice; mix well. Tint pale green with few drips green food coloring, if desired. Beat egg whites until stiff, but not dry; gradually add sugar and beat until very stiff. Fold into lime-milk mixture. Turn into ice tray; sprinkle edge with remaining crumbs. Place in freezer and chill until firm, about 6 hours.

Note: If desired, filling may be turned into a baked 8-inch pastry shell. Omit egg whites and sugar in filling to use for meringue. Beat egg whites until soft peaks are formed when beater is lifted; add sugar gradually, beating until stiff. Put on top of lime filling. Spread with spoon, being careful to spread meringue against edge of pastry shell. Bake in a moderate oven (350 degrees) 20 to 25 minutes.

4–6 servings.

Source: *Florida's Favorite Foods. Fruits and Vegetables in the Family Menu.* Bulletin No. 46, Tallahassee, FL: Florida Department of Agriculture, 1959.

Frozen Surprise

2 quarts drained bottled or canned citrus salad
1⅔ ounces (5 envelopes) unflavored gelatin
2 cups reserved syrup
1 cup mayonnaise
3 cups heavy cream or whipped topping
For garnish: Maraschino cherries and citrus sections

In saucepan, sprinkle gelatin over syrup to soften. Stir over low heat until gelatin is completely dissolved. Cool slightly. Whip cream or whip topping until almost stiff. In separate bowl, gradually blend gelatin mixture into mayonnaise; stir in whipped cream, blending thoroughly. Cut drained fruit coarsely. Fold into cream mixture quickly. Turn into 20 × 12× 2 pan. Cover tightly with plastic wrap or foil. Freeze. To serve: Remove from freezer about ½ hour before serving time. Lightly frost with additional whipped cream, cut into squares and garnish.

4 quarts, or 24 servings, 3½ × 3.

Source: *Chilled Florida Citrus Sections For Around the Year Profit.* CCS-1, Lakeland, FL: Florida Citrus Commission, no date.

Fruit Sherbet

¼ cup orange juice
½ cup lemon juice
2½ cups sugar
1 quart milk
1 cup any of the following crushed fruits: strawberries, peaches,
　　bananas, mangoes, guavas, papayas

Mix and freeze. If mixture curdles, it will freeze smooth again.

Source: *Florida Fruits and Vegetables in the Family Menu.* Bulletin No. 46, New Series, Tallahassee, FL: Florida Department of Agriculture, 1956.

Grapefruit Alaska

Cut 3 grapefruit in half, and using scissors cut out more of the core than usual; remove all seeds. Cut around each section to loosen, sprinkle with a little sugar and chill thoroughly. When ready to serve, put a scoop of mint, vanilla or other ice cream in center cavity of each grapefruit half, cover completely with meringue, place on baking sheet, and bake in a hot oven (450 degrees) about 5 minutes; then place under broiler for 1 minute to brown meringue. Serve immediately.

Meringue

3 egg whites
½ teaspoon salt
6 tablespoons sugar
1 teaspoon vanilla

Beat egg whites until foamy, add salt and beat until stiff, but not dry. Gradually beat in sugar until stiff and glossy. Stir in vanilla. Makes 6 servings.

Allow ½ grapefruit per person.

Source: *Using Florida Citrus Fruits.* Circular No. 231, Gainesville, FL: University of Florida Agricultural Extension Service, 1962.

Grapefruit Cream Sherbet

1 tablespoon gelatin
½ cup cold water
1½ cups sugar
1½ cups boiling water
Grated rind of 1 grapefruit
2 eggs
2 cups orange juice
1½ cups grapefruit juice
1 pint cream or evaporated milk
½ cup powdered sugar
Few grains salt

Soak gelatin in cold water for five minutes. Dissolve gelatin and 1 ½ cups sugar in boiling water. Add grapefruit rind, juice and orange juice. Place in mold next to ice, and harden to mush. Beat cream until stiff, add ½ cup sugar and salt. Separate yolks from whites. Beat yolks until foaming and whites until stiff. Combine, add to cream. Fold into the hardened mixture. Return to freezer or on top of ice. Stir this mixture twice during the freezing process.

Source: *Florida Fruits and Vegetables in the Family Menu.* Bulletin No. 46, New Series, Tallahassee, FL: Florida Department of Agriculture, 1956.

Grapefruit Halves

To prepare grapefruit halves: Cut fruit in half; remove core if desired. Cut around each section, loosening fruit from membrane. Do not cut around entire outer edge of fruit. Serve plain or with any of the following toppings:

Serve grapefruit halves with a spoonful of preserves, honey, or maple syrup.

Fill center with canned Bing cherries, or other fresh berries in season.

Cut out center of grapefruit; sprinkle lightly with sugar; chill. Make meringue, using 1 egg white for each 2 grapefruit halves. Put spoonful of vanilla ice cream in center of grapefruit; cover with meringue. Bake in hot oven (450 degrees) or broil a few seconds until delicately browned.

Place crushed maple sugar candy or peppermint candy in center of halves.

Source: *Florida Citrus Fare.* Lakeland, FL: Florida Citrus Commission, no date.

Grapefruit Rose

Cut a grapefruit in half, take out all the sections, skin them and cut in small pieces. Trim the edges of the hollow halves in pointed scallops. Combine the cut fruits with bits of orange, avocado pear, chipped apple or pear, and put the mixture into the trimmed grapefruit skins. Garnish with maraschino cherry or preserved ginger, also with a sprig of watercress and a little dab of mayonnaise.

Source: *Florida Fruits and Vegetables in the Family Menu.* Bulletin No. 46, New Series, Tallahassee, FL: Florida Department of Agriculture, 1956.

Grapefruit Sherbet

1 pint boiling water
4 cups grapefruit juice
2 teaspoons gelatin
2 tablespoons cold water
2 cups honey
Juice of 1 lemon
Shredded or candied orange peel

Soften gelatin in cold water. Add boiling water and honey. Stir until dissolved, cool, and add fruit juices. Cool and freeze in three parts of ice to one part of salt. Garnish each serving with shredded candied cherries or strips of candied orange peel.

Source: *Florida Honey and Its Hundred Uses.* Bulletin No. 66, Tallahassee, FL: Florida Department of Agriculture, 1955.

Grapefruit Souffle

1 cup milk
½ cup cutup grapefruit sections
3 tablespoons orange juice
½ cup sugar
½ tablespoon vanilla
4 tablespoons flour
4 tablespoons butter
1 tablespoon lemon juice
Grated rind of ½ orange

Make a white sauce of the flour, butter, and milk. Cool. Add the rest of the ingredients except the egg whites. Beat these very stiff and fold in last. Turn into buttered baking dish and bake at 325 degrees about one hour .

Source: *Florida Fruits and Vegetables in the Family Menu.* Bulletin No. 46, New Series, Tallahassee, FL: Florida Department of Agriculture, 1956.

Grapefruit Surprise

1 cup plus 3 tablespoons sugar, divided
¼ cup cornstarch
½ teaspoon salt
3 eggs, separated
2 cups milk
3 tablespoons butter or margarine
1 teaspoon vanilla
3 large grapefruit

In medium saucepan, combine 1 cup sugar, cornstarch and salt. Gradually add milk and egg yolks; mix well. Cook over low heat, stirring constantly until mixture boils. Boil 1 minute. Remove from heat. Stir in butter and vanilla. Cover surface of pudding with plastic wrap; chill.

Meanwhile, prepare grapefruit. Cut grapefruit in half. Using grapefruit knife, section fruit; drain. Remove all membrane from grapefruit shells. Fill grapefruit shells with sections. Spoon chilled pudding over sections.

In small bowl, beat egg whites until foamy. Gradually beat in remaining 3 tablespoons sugar, beating until stiff peaks form. Spoon or pipe meringue evenly over pudding.

Place grapefruit shells on cookie sheet. Place under broiler about 2 minutes until meringue is golden. Watch carefully to avoid burning. Serve immediately.

6 servings.

Source: *Willard Scott: My Favorite Florida Citrus Recipes.* Lakeland, FL: Florida Department of Citrus, no date.

Picking grapefruit in St. Petersburg, April 8, 1935. Floyd and Marion Rinhart Collection. Archives and Special Collections, University of Miami Library.

Grapefruit Whip

⅓ cup grapefruit pulp
⅓ cup powdered sugar
2 tablespoons currant jelly
1 egg white
1¼ cups chopped nut meats
3 tablespoons marshmallow creme
3 maraschino cherries, diced

Combine and beat grapefruit pulp, sugar, jelly, marshmallow creme, nuts, and cherries. Whip white until dry and stiff, and fold in first mixture. Serve immediately in sherbet glasses, garnishing top with whole Maraschino cherry. Ladyfingers, sponge cake, or vanilla wafers may be served with it, or with the whip laid in portions on each slice of cake or cookie.

Source: *Florida Fruits and Vegetables in the Family Menu.* Bulletin No. 46, New Series, Tallahassee, FL: Florida Department of Agriculture, 1956.

Grapefruit-Lime Ring Mold

1 3-ounce package cream cheese
1 cup boiling water
2 3-ounce packages lime-flavored gelatin
2 cups reserved grapefruit syrup
1 quart drained grapefruit sections
Maraschino cherries

Shape cheese into 8 balls; chill. In saucepan, add boiling water to gelatin and stir over low heat until completely dissolved. Add grapefruit syrup. In 5-cup ring mold, spoon gelatin mixture to cover bottom; arrange 8 grapefruit sections, cherries and cheese balls. Spoon in gelatin mixture slowly to barely cover fruit; chill until almost firm. Chill remaining gelatin mixture until syrupy; fold in remaining grapefruit. Spoon on top of first layer. Chill until firm. To serve: unmold on salad greens and fill center with additional fruit as desired.

Yields 1 5-cup or 12 3-ounce molds. For individual molds, prepare additional cheese balls. Mold grapefruit and cherries; decorate center with cheese ball.

Source: *Chilled Florida Citrus Sections For Around the Year Profit.* CCS-1, Lakeland, FL: Florida Citrus Commission, no date.

Guava Brown Betty

1 cup sugar
¼ teaspoon each cinnamon and nutmeg
2 cups bread crumbs
¼ cup water
3 tablespoons lemon or lime juice
2 cups guavas, seeded and cut in small pieces

Blend the sugar, spices, and lemon rind. Mix crumbs and butter lightly with fork. Cover bottom of buttered pudding dish with crumbs and add ½ of the guavas. Sprinkle with the sugared mixture; repeat, cover with remaining crumbs. Mix the water and lemon juice, and pour over. Dot with bits of butter and bake in a moderate oven (350 degrees) for 45 minutes. Cover at first to keep crumbs from browning too rapidly. Serve with cream (optional).

Serves about 8.

Source: *Growing and Preparing Guavas.* Bulletin No. 74, Tallahassee, FL: Florida Department of Agriculture, 1957.

Guava Ice Cream

Beat 2 egg yolks. Add ¼ cup cream and ¾ cup confectioners sugar. Cook in double boiler or over very slow flame, stirring constantly until slightly thickened. Chill. Add 2 cups stewed chopped guavas. Whip 1 cup heavy cream until stiff. In another bowl whip the 2 egg whites and ½ teaspoon salt until stiff. Fold the stiffly beaten cream and egg whites into the chilled custard and guavas. Freeze in ice trays. Top each serving with stewed chopped guavas and nuts or fresh, grated coconut.

Source: *Growing and Preparing Guavas.* Bulletin No. 74, Tallahassee, FL: Florida Department of Agriculture, 1957.

Guava Tapioca

¼ **cup quick-cooking tapioca**
1 **cup boiling water**
¼ **teaspoon cinnamon**
2 **tablespoons lime juice**
½ **cup sugar**
¼ **teaspoon salt**
2 **tablespoons butter**
3 **cups peeled, sliced, seeded guavas**

Add the boiling water to the tapioca and cook until it clears. Add sugar, cinnamon, salt, and fruit juice. Place the guavas in a greased shallow glass baking dish, dot with butter, and pour the tapioca mixture over them. Bake in a moderate oven until the guavas are tender and the top is slightly browned. Serve hot or cold with plain or whipped cream.

Source: *Growing and Preparing Guavas.* Bulletin No. 74, Tallahassee, FL: Florida Department of Agriculture, 1957.

Honey Kumquat Sauce

1 cup honey
½ to ¾ cup finely chopped fresh kumquats, seeded
1 cup orange juice
⅛ teaspoon salt
1 tablespoon butter (optional)

Combine the ingredients and let stand over hot water, without cooking, for about 30 minutes to blend the flavors. Serve as a sauce on ice cream.

Source: *Florida Honey and Its Hundred Uses.* Bulletin No. 66, Tallahassee, FL: Florida Department of Agriculture, 1955.

Banana plant and thatched hut at Seminole Indian Village, February 25, 1930. Floyd and Marion Rinhart Collection. Archives and Special Collections, University of Miami Library.

Honey Mousse

¼ cup powdered sugar
½ cup shredded pineapple (drained)
2 egg whites
½ cup honey (warmed)
½ cup candied orange peel or kumquat
1 cup cream (whipped)
1 teaspoon vanilla extract
½ cup pecans

Mix pineapple, honey, chopped nuts, peel, and flavoring. Cool. Beat the egg whites until stiff and add powdered sugar. Beat cream until fairly stiff. Fold all ingredients together and freeze either in cups or in ice trays.

Source: *Florida Honey and Its Hundred Uses.* Bulletin No. 66, Tallahassee, FL: Florida Department of Agriculture, 1933.

Honey Orange Strips

Remove the peel from three oranges in quarter sections, then cut into strips with scissors. Cover rind with saltwater in proportions of 1 tablespoon of salt to one quart of water and let stand overnight. Drain and cover with cold water, then bring to the boiling point; repeat process three times. Then if tender, rinse in cold water, drain, then simmer very slowly in 1 cup of honey from 45 to 60 minutes. Remove the rind with fork. Drain and lay on waxed paper. Allow to dry for a day or two. The strips may then be coated with chocolate if desired.

Source: *Florida Bees and Honey.* Bulletin No. 117, Tallahassee, FL: Florida Department of Agriculture, 1943.

Honey Strawberry Sherbet

1 pint strawberries
2 lemons
⅞ cup honey
2 cups water
1 egg white

Mix the strawberries (which have been put through a sieve), lemon juice, water, and honey and let stand several hours to blend. Put into a freezer and when it begins to freeze add beaten egg white. Freeze with 8 parts ice to 1 part salt and pack with 3 parts ice to 1 part salt.

Makes 1 quart.

Source: *Florida Honey and Its Hundred Uses.* Bulletin No. 66, Tallahassee, FL: Florida Department of Agriculture, 1955.

Honeyed Prunes

½ pound prunes
1½ cups boiling water
¼ cup honey
2 slices lemon

Wash and drain prunes. Cover with boiling water and let stand until cool. Add honey and lemon slices, place in covered container and keep in cool place till ready for use. The prunes may be boiled and strained through a sieve before being mixed with the honey, thus making a delightful spread.

Source: *Florida Bees and Honey.* Bulletin No. 117, Tallahassee, FL: Florida Department of Agriculture, 1943.

Lemon Sherbet

3 cups sugar
1 quart water
¾ cup lemon juice
2 egg whites

Boil sugar and water together for 5 minutes to make syrup. Add lemon juice, cool, and freeze to a mush. Add stiffly beaten egg whites and finish freezing.

Makes about 1¾ quarts.

Source: *Florida Fruits and Vegetables in the Family Menu.* Bulletin No. 46, New Series, Tallahassee, FL: Florida Department of Agriculture, 1956.

Lemon Sponge Pudding

¾ cup sugar
¼ cup flour
⅛ teaspoon melted butter or margarine
¼ cup lemon juice
½ teaspoon grated lemon rind
2 eggs, separated
1½ cups milk

Mix together sugar and flour. Add salt, shortening, lemon juice, and lemon rind. Beat egg yolks and add milk. Combine with sugar mixture. Beat egg whites until stiff but not dry, and fold into the mixture. Pour into greased custard cups or a baking dish, and set in a pan of hot water. Bake at 350 degrees (moderate oven) for 40 to 45 minutes.

Six ¼ cup servings.

Source: *Favorite Dairy Dishes.* Bulletin No. 181, Tallahassee, FL: Florida Department of Agriculture, 1959.

Lime Meringuettes

3 eggs, separated
¼ teaspoon cream of tartar
⅛ teaspoon salt
1 cup sugar
4 tablespoons lime juice
1½ teaspoons lime rind
1 cup heavy cream, whipped

Beat egg whites until foamy; add cream of tartar and salt; beat until stiff but not dry. Add ¾ cup of the sugar gradually, beating until very stiff. Cover baking sheet with heavy brown paper. Pile meringue into 6 rounds about 3 inches in diameter. Make a 2-inch depression in the center. Bake in a very slow oven (275 degrees) 1 hour. For the filling, beat the egg yolks; add remaining ¼ cup sugar and the lime juice. Cook over boiling water, stirring constantly until thickened. Add grated lime rind. Remove from heat; chill. Fold into whipped cream. Fill meringue shells. Chill 6 to 12 hours in refrigerator.

6 servings.

Source: *Florida Citrus Fare.* Lakeland, FL: Florida Citrus Commission, no date.

Mango Sundae

Have the fruit well chilled. Cut in halves and remove the seed. Fill the cavity with ice cream (plain vanilla is best), and serve at once.

Source: *Florida Fruits and Vegetables in the Family Menu.* Bulletin No. 46, New Series, Tallahassee, FL: Florida Department of Agriculture, 1956.

Mango Tarts

4 mangoes
1 cup sugar
½ cup water
2 tablespoons butter
1 teaspoon corn starch
2 beaten egg yolks
1 teaspoon cinnamon

Peel and slice thin the mangoes. Heat fruit in saucepan with sugar and water. When sauce has cooked for 15 minutes, add cornstarch that has been mixed with a little water and mixed with the 2 beaten egg yolks. Allow this to cook for several minutes, stirring constantly until thick and smooth. Stir in the teaspoon cinnamon and 2 table-

Lake Luzerne, Orlando, 1923. Floyd and Marion Rinhart Collection. Archives and Special Collections, University of Miami Library.

spoons butter. Fill already-baked patty shells or pastry tart shells with this mixture and serve cool.

Source: *Florida's Favorite Foods. Fruits and Vegetables in the Family Menu.* Bulletin No. 46, Tallahassee, FL: Florida Department of Agriculture, 1959.

Miami Grapefruit Ring Salad Mold

Grapefruit sections
Canned grapefruit juice
2 envelopes unflavored gelatin
¼ cup sugar
¼ teaspoon salt
1 3-ounce package cream cheese
½ cup diced celery
16 maraschino cherries

Drain grapefruit sections; measure syrup and add canned grapefruit juice to make 3 cups. Soften gelatin in 1 cup of the liquid. Heat remaining liquid; add to softened gelatin with sugar and salt; stir until dissolved. Chill until slightly thickened. Form cream cheese into small balls. Arrange balls and ½ cup cut grapefruit sections in 1½ quart ring mold. Cover with gelatin; chill until almost firm. Add 1 cup grapefruit sections with celery to remaining gelatin and turn into ring mold; chill. Unmold and fill center with cherries and remaining grapefruit sections.

10 servings.

Source: *Florida Citrus Fare.* Lakeland, FL: Florida Citrus Commission, no date.

Molded Citrus Dessert

1 envelope unflavored gelatin
1¾ cups canned tangerine, grapefruit, orange, or blended juice
4 tablespoons sugar
⅛ teaspoon salt
1½ cups canned grapefruit sections, well drained

Soften gelatin in ½ cup citrus juice. Heat remaining 1¼ cups juice; add gelatin, sugar and salt; stir until dissolved. Chill until slightly thickened. Fold in grapefruit sections. Chill in individual molds until firm. Unmold on crisp greens; serve with salad dressing, or as dessert with whipped cream.

6 servings.

Source: *Florida Citrus Fare.* Lakeland, FL: Florida Citrus Commission, no date.

Orange Bread Pudding

3 slices stale bread
2 eggs
½ cup sugar
¼ teaspoon salt
1⅔ cups milk
1 cup orange juice
1 teaspoon grated or finely chopped orange rind

Cut bread in small cubes or break into small pieces. Place in buttered baking dish. Beat eggs. Add sugar, salt, and milk to eggs. Stir in orange juice and rind. Pour mixture over bread. Bake in a moderate oven (350 degrees) until set, about 45 minutes.

6–8 servings.

Source: *Using Florida Citrus Fruits.* Circular No. 231, Gainesville, FL: University of Florida Agricultural Extension Service, 1962.

Orange Custard

2 cups milk
2 eggs, beaten
1 cup sugar
2 tablespoons cornstarch
1 teaspoon butter
⅛ teaspoon salt
2 tablespoons lime juice
6 oranges, sectioned

Mix sugar and cornstarch and add cold milk. Add beaten eggs. Cook over hot water until thick. Remove from heat. Add butter, salt, and lime juice. Cool. Place orange sections in sherbet glasses. Pour custard over oranges and top with whipped cream.

6 servings.

Source: *Using Florida Citrus Fruits.* Circular No. 231, Gainesville, FL: University of Florida Agricultural Extension Service, 1962.

Orange Frappe

2 cups sugar
3 cups water
2 cups orange juice
½ cup lemon juice

Boil sugar and water 10 minutes. Cool, add fruit juices. Freeze to a mush.

Source: *Florida Fruits and Vegetables in the Family Menu.* Bulletin No. 46, New Series, Tallahassee, FL: Florida Department of Agriculture, 1956.

THIS twenty-pound package of assorted Grape Fruit, Oranges, Tangarines and Kumquats will be sent to your address by prepaid express for $_____

All orders shipped same day received. All fruit picked fresh every morning. All orders cash.

HICKSON & WHITENER
MIAMI, FLORIDA

REFERENCES: ANY BANK IN MIAMI

Hickson & Whitener twenty-pound package. New York: Valentine Souvenier Co., no date. Florida Postcard Collection. Archives and Special Collections., University of Miami Library.

Orange Ice Cream

3 cups orange juice
1 cup sugar
1 cup heavy cream
2 cups light cream or milk

Mix orange juice and sugar thoroughly. Add cream and milk and freeze. Or add just thin cream or milk, freeze to a mush; add whipped cream and continue freezing.

Source: *Florida Fruits and Vegetables in the Family Menu.* Bulletin No. 46, New Series, Tallahassee, FL: Florida Department of Agriculture, 1956.

Orange Ripple Sherbet

¼ cup cold water
1 envelope unflavored gelatin
1½ cups light corn syrup
2 cups milk
1 6-ounce can orange concentrate, thawed
1 6-ounce package semi-sweet chocolate bits
2 tablespoons salad oil

Soften gelatin in cold water, heat to melt. Add syrup, milk, and undiluted concentrate. Blend. Pour into tray and freeze until just frozen. Melt chocolate bits over hot water, add salad oil and beat. Beat frozen mixture in a chilled bowl until smooth but not melted. Return to tray and quickly drizzle in chocolate. Stir to ripple and return to coldest part of freezing unit. Freeze until firm. Serve in chilled dishes. For plain sherbet, omit chocolate and salad oil.

Serves 8.

Source: *Using Florida Citrus Fruits.* Circular No. 231, Gainesville, FL: University of Florida Agricultural Extension Service, 1962.

Orange Snow

1 tablespoon gelatin
¼ cup cold water
¼ cup hot water
¼ cup sugar
¼ teaspoon salt
1 cup orange juice
3 medium oranges, sectioned
1 tablespoon lime juice
2 egg whites, beaten until stiff

Soften gelatin in cold water. Add hot water and stir until dissolved. Add sugar, salt, fruit juices, and fruit sections cut into small pieces; mix thoroughly. Cool. When mixture begins to thicken, beat until frothy. Fold in stiffly beaten egg whites. Turn into mold that has been rinsed in cold water. Chill until firm. Unmold and garnish with orange slices and strawberries.

6 servings.

Source: *Using Florida Citrus Fruits.* Circular No. 231, Gainesville, FL: University of Florida Agricultural Extension Service, 1962.

Orange Supreme

To a large scoop of vanilla ice cream served in a chilled champagne glass, add 2 or 3 wedges of orange or tangerine evenly spaced around sides. Mix one small can orange juice concentrate with two table-spoons of Countreau and ladle over ice cream. Garnish with shred-ded coconut.

Source: *Famous Florida Chefs' Favorite Citrus Recipes.* Lakeland, FL: Florida Citrus Commission, no date.

Orange Tapioca

1½ cups water
½ cup sugar
¼ teaspoon salt
⅓ cup quick-cooking tapioca
1 cup orange or other citrus juice
1 teaspoon grated or finely chopped orange rind
½ cup evaporated milk, thoroughly chilled
2 teaspoons lime juice

Bring water, sugar, and salt to a boil in top of double boiler. Add tapioca and bring to brisk boil, stirring constantly. Place over boiling water and cook 5 minutes longer, stirring occasionally. Cool. Add orange juice and rind. When mixture is cold, whip the chilled milk, add lime juice, and fold into the pudding.

8 servings.

Source: *Using Florida Citrus Fruits.* Circular No. 231, Gainesville, FL: University of Florida Agricultural Extension Service, 1962.

Papaya Milk Sherbet

1½ cups ripe papaya pulp
3 tablespoons lemon juice
½ cup orange juice
1½ cups milk
1 cup sugar

Press papaya pulp through a coarse sieve and combine with fruit juice. Dissolve sugar in milk, add fruit mixture gradually to milk, and freeze in an ice cream freezer, using 8 parts of ice to 1 part of ice cream salt. Ice cream may be made by substituting light cream for milk.

Source: *The Papaya. A Fruit Suitable for South Florida.* Bulletin No. 90, New Series, Tallahassee, FL: Florida Department of Agriculture, 1939.

Papaya Sherbet

Mix four cups papaya pulp with two cups sugar and juice of three lemons and freeze.

Source: *Florida Fruits and Vegetables in the Family Menu.* Bulletin No. 46, New Series, Tallahassee, FL: Florida Department of Agriculture, 1956.

Persimmon Ice

2 tablespoons of gelatin
1¾ cups sugar
1 pint boiling water
1½ pints of grapefruit juice
1½ pints of persimmon pulp (riced or run through a colander)

Soak gelatin 5 minutes in ½ cup of cold water, adding the boiling water and sugar, stir well and let cool, then add the grapefruit juice and freeze until like mush. Fold in the peeled and riced persimmons and continue freezing until firm. Pack and allow the ice to stand for several hours before serving. In making persimmon ice, special care should be used to select thoroughly ripe fruit.

Source: *Florida Fruits and Vegetables in the Family Menu.* Bulletin No. 46, New Series, Tallahassee, FL: Florida Department of Agriculture, 1956.

Persimmon Ice Cream

Beat together thoroughly 2 cups of persimmon pulp, 1 cup sugar and one cup of thick, sweet cream, and freeze in a rotary freezer. The fruit must be thoroughly ripe.

Source: *Florida Fruits and Vegetables in the Family Menu.* Bulletin No. 46, New Series, Tallahassee, FL: Florida Department of Agriculture, 1956.

Pineapple Dessert

4 cups shredded pineapple
12 marshmallows
Strawberry jam
Whipped cream

In each dessert glass put a layer of shredded pineapple, then 2 marshmallows, cut in pieces with scissors dipped in cold water. Next a layer of jam, another layer of shredded pineapple. Top with whipped cream, sweetened and flavored. Sprinkle with chopped nuts or coconut.

Source: *Florida Fruits and Vegetables in the Family Menu.* Bulletin No. 46, New Series, Tallahassee, FL: Florida Department of Agriculture, 1956.

Pineapple with Orange Sections

1 slice fresh pineapple
Powdered sugar
Orange sections

Chill pineapple and orange. Peel orange with a sharp knife, cutting through the white inner skin. Remove sections, keeping in as large pieces as possible. When ready to serve, lay slices of pineapple on individual plates, put a small mound of powdered sugar in the center and arrange orange sections around pineapple slices, making a complete circle. Serve cold.

Source: *Florida Fruits and Vegetables in the Family Menu.* Bulletin No. 46, New Series, Tallahassee, FL: Florida Department of Agriculture, 1956.

Quick Orange Pudding

1 package instant vanilla pudding mix
2 cups orange juice, fresh, frozen, or canned
½ cup cream for whipping
½ cup orange sections
1 teaspoon grated orange rind

Follow directions on package forpudding, using orange juice in place of milk. Add sections and rind. Spoon into serving dishes. Chill. Before serving, top with whipped cream.

Serves 4-6.

Source: *Using Florida Citrus Fruits.* Circular No. 231, Gainesville, FL: University of Florida Agricultural Extension Service, 1962.

Rainbow Ambrosia

Arrange orange and grapefruit sections in a sherbet glass. Garnish with strawberries and coconut. Pour 1½ to 2 ounces of cream sherry over fruit.

Source: *Chilled Florida Citrus Sections For Around the Year Profit.* CCS-1, Lakeland, FL: Florida Citrus Commission, no date.

South Florida Freeze

6 cups grated coconut (2 large coconuts), or 4¼ cups extracted coconut milk
½ teaspoon vanilla
3½ cups boiling water
⅞ cup coconut water
1¼ cups sugar

Pour the boiling water over the grated coconut and allow to stand 15 minutes. Strain through a double thickness of cheesecloth squeezing out as much as possible. Add the coconut water, sugar, and vanilla to the extracted coconut milk, and stir until the sugar is dissolved. Freeze in an ice cream freezer, using 8 parts of ice to 1 part of ice cream salt. Grated coconut may be served over the frozen mixture.

Source: *Florida Fruits and Vegetables in the Family Menu.* Bulletin No. 46, New Series, Tallahassee, FL: Florida Department of Agriculture, 1956.

Southern Classique

Prepare a basic ambrosia mixture of orange and grapefruit sections, shredded or flaked coconut, and pineapple or other desired fruit. Top with whipped cream or soft ice cream. Garnish with additional coconut and cherries.

Source: *Chilled Florida Citrus Sections For Around the Year Profit.* CCS-1, Lakeland, FL: Florida Citrus Commission, no date.

Tangerine Ice Suckers

1 6-ounce can frozen tangerine concentrate
16 to 18 popsickle sticks

Thaw concentrate and pour into an ice tray. Place in freezer. When partially frozen, insert sticks. Finish freezing. When completely frozen remove from tray and place in plastic bag. Seal with rubber band and keep in freezer unit until used.

Source: *Using Florida Citrus Fruits.* Circular No. 231, Gainesville, FL: University of Florida Agricultural Extension Service, 1962.

Tangerine Served "As Is" for Dessert

Cut tangerine peel in six sections; peel down part of the way and tuck in peel against sections. Spread the sections apart sunburst-fashion. Fill center with raisins or salted nuts.

Source: *Florida Citrus Fare.* Lakeland, FL: Florida Citrus Commission, no date.

Pies

Blueberry Tarts

Fresh blueberries
Powdered sugar
Tart shells
Whipped cream

The pastry is made by mixing 1 cup flour, ¼ teaspoon baking powder, and ⅜ teaspoon salt, cutting in 6 tablespoons of shortening and adding enough water to make a soft dough. Place dough on floured board, work, and roll out to fit tart shells. Bake in a moderate oven for about 25 minutes.

After tart shells have been removed from oven, allow to cool, fill shells with blueberries, sprinkle with powdered sugar and cover with whipped cream.

Source: *Florida Blueberries.* Bulletin No. 13-B, New Series, Tallahassee, FL: Florida Department of Agriculture, 1950.

Citrus Tarts

2 cups canned or fresh tangerine, orange, blended,
    or grapefruit juice
1 package vanilla pudding
6 baked tart shells
Whipped cream
Citrus sections

Use any of the canned or fresh citrus juices as the liquid in preparing vanilla pudding. Chill; fill tart shells. Garnish with whipped cream and citrus sections.

6 tarts.

Source: *Florida Citrus Fare.* Lakeland, FL: Florida Citrus Commission, no date.

Harvesting the Coconuts. Copyright, 1891, by George Barker. Floyd and Marion Rinhart Collection. Archives and Special Collections, University of Miami Library.

Coconut-Sweet Potato Pie

1 cup shredded coconut
1½ cups mashed sweet potatoes
¾ cup sugar
¾ cup milk
½ cup water
½ teaspoon cinnamon
½ teaspoon allspice
2 tablespoons melted butter
2 eggs, slightly beaten

Mix the above ingredients and pour into a pan lined with unbaked pastry. Bake in a moderate oven.

Source: *Florida Fruits and Vegetables in the Family Menu.* Bulletin No. 46, New Series, Tallahassee, FL: Florida Department of Agriculture, 1956.

Favorite Coconut Cream Pie

2 cups milk
3 egg yolks
¾ cup sugar
¹⁄₁₆ teaspoon salt
3 tablespoons cornstarch
½ teaspoon vanilla
½ cup whipping cream
¾ cup fresh grated coconut

Combine the sugar, cornstarch, and salt. Scald the milk and add the dry ingredients slowly to the hot milk, stirring until a smooth mixture is obtained. Cook over hot water, stirring frequently. Cool the mixture to lukewarm and stir in the egg yolks. Cook over hot water until the custard thickens. Cool, add vanilla, and pour into a baked pie shell. Chill and whip the cream. Just before serving spread the custard with the whipped cream and sprinkle with coconut.

Source: *Florida's Favorite Foods. Fruits and Vegetables in the Family Menu.* Bulletin No. 46, Tallahassee, FL: Florida Department of Agriculture, 1959.

Grapefruit Meringue Pie

1 cup sugar
Juice of ½ grapefruit
1 cup boiling water
2 tablespoons flour
¼ tablespoon melted butter
3 to 6 tablespoons sugar for meringue

Mix flour, sugar, and salt, and add boiling water gradually, stirring constantly. Add butter and cook 15 minutes over hot water. Add grapefruit juice and beaten yolks of eggs, stirring the eggs in quickly. Remove from the fire. Cool and turn into a baked crust. Cover with a meringue made from the stiffly beaten egg whites and sugar. Brown in a slow oven.

Source: *Florida Fruits and Vegetables in the Family Menu.* Bulletin No. 46, New Series, Tallahassee, FL: Florida Department of Agriculture, 1956.

Honey Lemon Pie

¾ cup honey
8 tablespoons flour
½ cup cold water
1 cup boiling water
1 lemon juice and grated rind
2 egg yolks
½ to 1 tablespoon butter

Blend the flour and cold water until smooth; add the honey and grated lemon rind; slowly add the boiling water, stirring constantly. Cook in a double boiler until thick. Stir in the lemon juice. Slowly add part of this cooked mixture to the beaten yolks, stirring constantly. Return to the double boiler and heat until the egg is cooked. Lastly, add the butter. Pour this filling into a baked pie crust and cover with a meringue made from the two egg whites slightly sweetened with honey and flavored with a drop or two of lemon extract. Brown meringue in the oven.

Source: *Florida Honey and Its Hundred Uses.* Bulletin No. 66, Tallahassee, FL: Florida Department of Agriculture, 1933.

Key Lime Tart

1 cup cake flour
1 teaspoon baking powder
1¾ ounce package instant lemon pudding
½ cup butter, softened
1 cup sugar
1 teaspoon lime peel, grated
1 teaspoon lemon extract
1 egg
½ cup milk
½ pint strawberries sliced confectioners sugar, sifted

Combine flour, baking powder, and dry pudding mix; set aside. Cream together butter and sugar; add lime peel and extract. Beat egg into batter mixture. Alternately add dry ingredients and milk into batter mixture, starting and ending with dry ingredients. Bake in pan at 350 degrees for 30 minutes. Cool slightly and invert on cake dish.

Filling

1 cup sugar
3 tablespoons cornstarch
1 cup cold water
3 egg yolks, slightly beaten
1 lime peel, grated
Juice of 1 lime
1 tablespoons butter

Mix sugar and cornstarch in saucepan. Add cold water slowly, stirring to prevent lumps. Add egg yolks and stir until mixed. Cook over medium heat until thickened, then boil one additional minute. Add last four ingredients, stir and cool.

Sprinkle outside edges of cake with sifted confectioners' sugar. Pour lime filling in indented center. Arrange sliced strawberries attractively on top of the lime mixture. Refrigerate until ready to serve.

6–8 servings.

Source: *Florida Holiday Recipes.* Tallahassee, FL: Florida Department of Agriculture and Consumer Services, 1990.

Lemon Fluff Pie

3 eggs
⅓ cup lemon juice
Grated rind of 1 lemon
3 tablespoons hot water
¼ teaspoon salt
1 cup sugar

Beat yolks of eggs until very light. Add lemon juice and grated rind, hot water, salt, and ½ cup sugar. Cook in double boiler until thick. Add ½ cup sugar to stiffly beaten egg whites and fold into cooked mixture. Fill baked pie shell and brown in moderate oven (350 degrees).

Source: *Florida's Favorite Foods. Fruits and Vegetables in the Family Menu.* Bulletin No. 46, Tallahassee, FL: Florida Department of Agriculture, 1959.

Field of strawberries near Plant City, FL, 1928. Floyd and Marion Rinhart Collection. Archives and Special Collections, University of Miami Library.

Lime Meringue Pie

4 tablespoons cornstarch
¾ cup sugar
¼ teaspoon salt
1¼ cups water
3 egg yolks
1 tablespoon butter or margarine
2 tablespoons grated lime rind
6 tablespoons lime juice
1 8-inch baked pastry shell

Blend cornstarch, sugar and salt in top double boiler. Stir in water. Cook over direct heat, stirring constantly, until mixture is very thick and transparent. Place over hot water; cover and cook 10 minutes. Beat egg yolks; add hot mixture, stirring rapidly. Return to double boiler and cook over hot water 3 minutes, stir constantly. Remove from heat; stir in butter, lime juice, and rind. Turn into baked pastry shell and top with meringue. Bake in moderate oven (375 degrees) 10 to 12 minutes.

To make meringue: Beat 3 egg whites until they form rounded peaks. Add gradually 6 tablespoons sugar, beating constantly until mixture is stiff and glossy.

1 8-inch pie.

Source: *Florida's Favorite Foods. Fruits and Vegetables in the Family Menu.* Bulletin No. 46, Tallahassee, FL: Florida Department of Agriculture, 1959.

Orange Bavarian Cream

1 tablespoon granulated gelatin
¼ cup cold water
1 cup orange juice pulp
1 tablespoon lime juice
½ cup sugar
Sprinkling salt
1 cup cream

Soak gelatin in cold water for 5 minutes and dissolve by standing cup containing mixture in hot water. Add to orange juice and pulp. Add lime juice, sugar and salt. When it begins to gel, fold in whipped cream; turn into cold mold to become firm.

Orange Bavarian Cream Pie

Make Orange Bavarian cream as given in recipe, pouring into baked pastry shell. Chill until firm. Top with additional whipped cream if desired.

Source: *Florida Fruits and Vegetables in the Family Menu.* Bulletin No. 46, New Series, Tallahassee, FL: Florida Department of Agriculture, 1956.

Orange Coconut Pie

1 baked deep 9-inch pastry shell
1 8-ounce can sweetened condensed milk
1⅓ cups orange sections and juice (3 oranges)
½ fresh coconut, coarsely grated
⅓ cup lime juice (2 limes)
4 eggs, separated
4 tablespoons sugar

Combine condensed milk, lime juice, and orange juice and fruit in a bowl. Stir until mixture thickens. Add 1 egg yolk at a time, beating well after each addition. Stir about ½ coconut in the mixture. Pour into cooled baked pastry shell. Beat egg whites until almost stiff enough to hold a peak. Add sugar gradually and continue beating until glossy but not dry. Pile meringue lightly on pie filling. Sprinkle coconut on top. Bake about 15 minutes at 325 degrees.

Source: *Florida's Favorite Recipes for Citrus Fruits. A compilation of recipes which won top honors in county contests jointly sponsored by the Florida Agricultural Extension Service, home demonstration work, and the Florida Chain Store Council as a feature of Florida's "Eat More Citrus Month," February, 1954.* Lakeland, FL: Florida Citrus Commission, 1954.

Orange Cream Pie

1 envelope unflavored gelatin
¼ teaspoon salt
⅓ cup sugar
1¾ cups orange juice
2 egg yolks
2 tablespoons lime juice
Grated rind of 2 oranges (about 2 tablespoons)
2 egg whites
¼ teaspoon cream of tartar
⅓ cup sugar
1 cup heavy cream, whipped
9-inch pie shell, baked

Combine gelatin, salt and sugar. Beat together orange juice and egg yolks; add to gelatin mixture. Cook over low heat, stirring constantly, until gelatin is dissolved and mixture is slightly thickened, about 5 minutes. Remove from heat and stir in lime juice and orange rind. Chill, stirring occasionally, until mixture is just beginning to set. Beat egg whites and cream of tartar until frothy. Gradually beat in sugar, a little at a time. Continue beating until stiff. Fold egg whites into gelatin mixture. Fold in whipped cream. Blend thoroughly. Pour into pie shell and chill until firm.

Source: *Florida Recipes*. Tallahassee, FL: Florida Department of Agriculture and Consumer Services, no date.

Orange Custard Tart

1⅓ cups flour, unsifted
½ cup plus 1 tablespoon sugar, divided
½ cup butter or margarine, softened
6 egg yolks, divided, slightly beaten
3 oranges, cut in wheels, seeds removed
⅓ cup orange marmalade
½ cup plus 1 tablespoon orange juice
3 tablespoons cornstarch
1 cup light cream or half and half
1 teaspoon orange peel, grated

Preheat oven to 400 degrees. In a medium-size bowl, mix flour and ¼ cup sugar, add butter and 2 egg yolks, and stir until mixture forms a ball. Press dough into 9-inch tart pan with removable bottom. Chill 15 minutes. Bake 10 minutes, reduce oven to 350 degrees, bake 10 to 15 minutes more, or until shell is lightly browned. Cool completely on wire rack, reserve. In a medium saute pan, heat marmalade and 1 tablespoon orange juice. Add orange slices, a few at a time, and cook 20 to 25 seconds, glazing each side. Transfer slices to plate when glazed, chill and reserve. In a small sauce pan, mix remaining sugar and cornstarch, gradually stir in cream over low heat until very thick. Beat cream mixture into remaining egg yolks and return to sauce pan. Stir in remaining orange juice and orange peel, and simmer over low heat until thickened, about 5 minutes. Place a piece of plastic wrap or parchment directly on surface of filling and chill well. To assemble, spread custard evenly in tart shell. Top with glazed orange wheels arranged in a spoke-like design. Chill, garnish with mint sprigs. Best when served within 3 hours of assembly.

To make citrus wheels: Slice fruit as many times as needed to create desired width. Cut away a small section of rind in a straight line from each slice. Rotate slices while cutting off rind six times to complete each citrus wheel.

Source: *Florida Citrus Sampler.* Lakeland, FL: Florida Department of Citrus, no date.

Orange Meringue Pie

1 cup sugar
5 tablespoons cornstarch or flour
1 teaspoon grated orange rind
1 cup orange juice
1 cup orange pulp
3 egg yolks, beaten
2 tablespoons lemon juice
2 tablespoons butter or margarine

Combine sugar, cornstarch or flour, grated orange rind, orange juice, and orange pulp. Cook on low heat or over hot water until clear. Add beaten egg yolks and cook about 5 minutes longer. Remove from heat. Blend in lemon juice and butter or margarine. Pour into a baked pie shell. Be sure filling and shell are both cold or both hot.

Meringue

3 egg whites
6 tablespoons sugar
¼ teaspoon lemon extract

Beat egg whites until stiff. Beat in sugar and lemon extract slowly until smooth and glossy. Spread on pie. Bake in a moderate oven, 350 degrees, until lightly browned.

Source: *Florida's Favorite Recipes for Citrus Fruits. A compilation of recipes which won top honors in county contests jointly sponsored by the Florida Agricultural Extension Service, home demonstration work, and the Florida Chain Store Council as a feature of Florida's "Eat More Citrus Month," February, 1954.* Lakeland, FL: Florida Citrus Commission, 1954.

Pineapples at Lake Worth, FL, no date. Floyd and Marion Rinhart Collection. Archives and Special Collections, University of Miami Library.

Papaya Pie

2 cups strained papaya pulp
1 tablespoon butter
2 egg yolks
¼ cup sugar
1 teaspoon ground cinnamon
¼ teaspoon ground nutmeg
1 teaspoon salt
2 tablespoons lemon juice (may be omitted)

Melt butter, add cooked papaya pulp, egg yolks, sugar, spices, and lemon juice. Pour into a baked pie shell. Bake for 45 minutes or until firm in moderate oven (325 degrees).

Source: *The Papaya. A Fruit Suitable for South Florida.* Bulletin No. 90, New Series, Tallahassee, FL: Florida Department of Agriculture, 1939.

Persimmon Cream Pie

3 very soft persimmons
2 eggs
2 cups milk or light cream
½ cup sugar
⅛ teaspoon of salt

Wash the persimmons and put through a ricer or rub through a colander. Beat the egg, add the sugar and salt and mix well. Add the cream or milk and the mashed persimmons. Pour into a partly baked pie crust, dot 4 tablespoonsfuls of butter over the top, and finish baking in a moderate oven (375 degrees) until the custard is set.

Source: *Florida Fruits and Vegetables in the Family Menu.* Bulletin No. 46, New Series, Tallahassee, FL: Florida Department of Agriculture, 1956.

Tampa Grapefruit Pie

1 9-inch pastry shell, baked
1 envelope unflavored gelatin
⅓ cup sugar
⅛ teaspoon salt
½ cup cold water
½ cup grapefruit juice
2 cups grapefruit sections, drained, cut into pieces
½ cup heavy cream, whipped

In medium saucepan, combine gelatin, sugar, and salt. Stir in water and grapefruit juice. Let stand 1 minute. Stir over low heat until gelatin is completely dissolved, about 5 minutes. Chill until slightly thickened. Add grapefruit sections to ¾ of the gelatin mixture; spoon

Orange Grove, Seville, FL, no date. Floyd and Marion Rinhart Collection. Archives and Special Collections, University of Miami Library.

into prepared pastry shell. Fold whipped cream to remaining gelatin mixture. Spoon over grapefruit layer. Chill until firm.

One 9-inch pie.

Source: *Willard Scott: My Favorite Florida Citrus Recipes.* Lakeland, FL: Florida Department of Citrus, no date.

INDEX

GRAPES

GUAVAS

PAPAYAS

PASTA